CONSCIOUS CREATIVITY

Ancient Europe's Mindfulness Meditations

Art of eLements

Nataša Pantović

AoL Mindfulness Book #7

ISBN-13: 978-99957-54-11-2

Published by: Artof4Elements

The Art of 4 Elements

○ △ □ ◎

https://www.artof4elements.com/
Printed 2015, Released 2019

DEDICATION

To the artists and musicians from around the world who continue to be my endless source of creative inspiration. Your work transcends boundaries, igniting the spark of imagination and reminding us all of the transformative power of art and music in our lives.

INTRODUCTON

It was during the Renaissance that creativity was first seen, not as a matter of divine inspiration, but as a gift of a great learned man to imitate God's ability to create. As Prometheus once stole fire from Gods to gift it to the mankind, humanity has stolen the essence of 'creation' from Gods.

Moving from imitating and copying, to innovating using our talents takes time. First we master a particular skill: a musician knows the rhythm, an architect understands engineering concepts, an artist learns about shades. Then we open our minds to the possibility of being different accepting our uniqueness.

PLATO CAVE

In Plato's cave, prisoners are chained in a cave facing a wall, unable to turn their heads. Imagine, walking down a long dark cave that is turned into prison. Imagine at the end of it, you come across a wall in front of which on a stone bench sit people chained to each other and chained to the bench and they sit there living their lives day after day not being able to turn or move. Behind them burns a fire and puppeteers hold the puppets that cast shadows on the wall of the cave. The prisoners look at the shadows, observe their movements, believing that what they see is real. A shadow of a book is a book for them, a shadow of a chair is a chair for them and because that is the only reality that exists for them - they believe in it full-heartedly.

And after you have imagined all of this ask yourself: How much time in life I spend really feeling, seeing, hearing, tasting - really living, and how much do I spend observing the movements of the shadows on the wall in front of me?

How many hours of the day we spend passively chained to the chairs of our choosing and how many we spend running in the woods?

Can we Learn Creativity?

Personal Development is a life-style. It starts with a million dollars question: Who am I? and it develops into 100s of creativity and transformations tools that we use during our day to reach our highest potential.

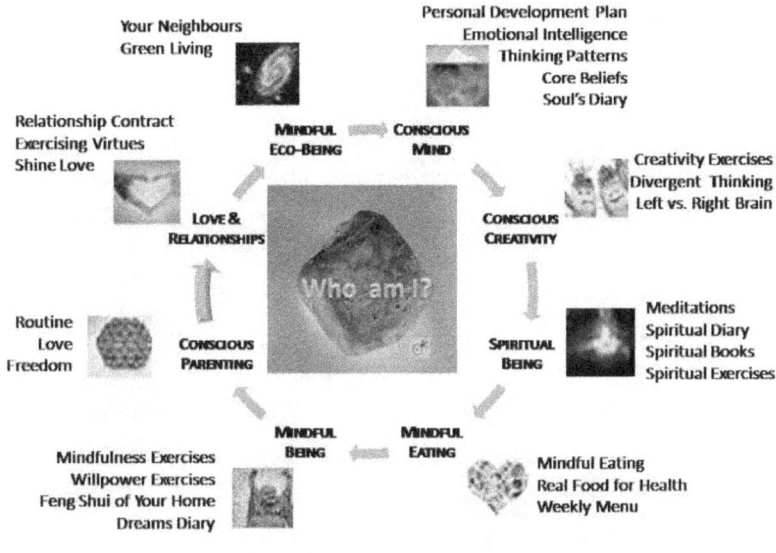

AoL Mind Map from Mindful Being Course, designed by Natasa Pantovic

I as an individual, or a social being, a lover, or a mother, a neighbour, or an inhabitant of Gaia... Who am I? The micro-cosmos and macro-cosmos of my existence faces this amazing web called: Life.

Balancing 4 Elements: intuition, thinking, emotions, sensation

The four elements within each one of us are: air, earth, fire, and water, four states of matter Life chooses to manifest on Earth. Jung describes them as four basic components of a personality: intuition, sensation, thinking and feeling.

Balancing our female and male side, our loving, meditative, artistic and intuitive Self with our intellectual, active and social Self is what you might have already experienced as a definition of completeness and happiness.

Sages and gurus of our past talk about this balance. Taoists with their concept of Yin and Yang, Yogis with their belief in two opposite energy forces entitled "Ida and Pingala", Jung that has studied the four components of personality as two pairs of opposites: sensations vs. intuition and thinking vs. feeling; Alchemists with their call to unite the opposites of: Venus and Mars, and Kabbalists with their ancient wisdom key called: Tree of Life, all reflect the dance of symbols and opposites.

Deeper comprehending the side of us that is ruled by instincts, habits and someone else's beliefs is the first step towards more complex co-existence on Earth.

Our Soul is the true driver of the chariot called body and mind, and as a source of inner knowing has been mentioned since Forever.

Magic of Human Brain

Albert Einstein 'I must be willing to give up what I am, in order to become what I will be.'

Ancient Xa in Modern Practices around the World

Within the spiritual growth arena, in our drive for goodness, humanity used to exercise tremendous efforts to transform Yin into Yang, searching for Balance within Order, applying force to guard "chastity", "honor", or "inner laws".

Within our understanding of the "wisdom" system, like in any learning, we pass through a spiral, slowly climbing up its various levels – physically, mentally and intuitively mastering the tools, comprehending its more subtle wisdom and beauty. Exercising Tai Chi, for example, takes us into a journey that as a gift combines breathing, movement, and the energy flow.

In Search of Happiness, following Ancient Greeks

Aristotel about eXellence (εὐδαιμονία)

The central concept of Aristotel's philosophy is within the words: Eudaimonia (Greek: εὐδαιμονία), that consists of the words 'eu' = 'good' + 'δ' + 'αιμονία' or 'aretē' that means 'done with excellence'.

Going back in time, just as a game, translating backwards with H (hidden by priests) + 'J'='Y' + the Slavic Cyrillic 'δ', 'B' that in Latin became 'D' = 'baimōn' 'blessed by the Amon's spirit of 'B''.

Aristotel in Nicomachean Ethics says '...if any action is well performed it is performed in accord with the appropriate 'excellence': if this is the case, then 'εὐδαιμονία' turns out to be an activity of the soul that is in-tuned with virtue.'

According to Aristotle, 'εὐδαιμονία' (wellbeing or long-term happiness) is achieved when during the life-time a human being achieves health, wealth, knowledge, friends and this in turn leads to the perfection of human nature. For Aristotle, 'εὐδαιμονία' involves activity, exhibiting 'aretē' (excellence) in accordance with reason.

'εὐδαιμονία' implies a divine state of being that a human being is able to achieve.

Confucius also sees the 'true happiness' first within an individual, then within a family and finally within a society. His wise words resonate within all of us:

'To put the world in order, we must first put the nation in order; to put the nation in order, we must first put the family in order; to put the family in order; we must first cultivate our personal life; we must first set our hearts right.' **Confucius about True Individual, Family and Social Happiness**

'Knowing others is intelligence; knowing yourself is true wisdom. Mastering others is strength; mastering yourself is true power. If you realize that you have enough, you are truly rich.' **Lao Tzu, Tao Te Ching About True Happiness**

'For every one step that you take in the pursuit of higher knowledge, take three steps in the perfection of your own character.' **Steiner about Human Character and Happiness**

Our alphabet comes from the Arabic speaking Phoenicians in the 800 BC through the Ancient Greece, so all the Ancient Egyptian translations have already lost or have hidden many sounds.

According to Ancient Greece Myths Zeus had many kids, Gods that have protected various cities of Mesopotamia:

Hephaistos, landed on the island of Lemnos, now Italy, becoming a master of fire, metallurgy, and crafts, a blacksmith building houses, armor, and ingenious devices. His workshop was on the Mt. Etna that erupted in Sicily so it allowed the development of metallurgy.

Athena his most favored daughter, is a founder Goddess of the Greek city of Athens with its first public schools, art centres, etc.

Zeus was also regarded as the founder of Macedonians, the Ancient Greek tribe that had Alexander the Great as their King. We have heard of him, going to Egypt with Aristotle, setting up Babylon as his Capital city.

Minos, Rhadamanthys & Sarpedon – are kids with Europa after Zeus took her to Crete.

Minoan Crete goes back to at least 7,000 BC with their legends, architecture and most amazing temples.

The Minoans were famous for its culture around 2000 BC, and they were a sophisticated political and trading force within Ancient Mediterranean Europe / North Africa.

The archaeological findings now suggest that their grand buildings were two stories high, decorated with fine frescoes, large courts, staircases, religious offerings, city-wells, drainage systems, extensive storage magazines to store wine, oil, grain, precious metals, and ceramics, and even 'theatre' areas for public spectacles. These all were centrally administrated by their Governors.

The lack of fortification walls suggests that they used travelling to trade not to war against one another. Within the Minoan religion they worshipped bulls. The eruption of the volcano on the island of Thera (today Santorini) in 1650 BC, and the resulting tsunami, is acknowledged as the final cause for the fall of the Minoans.

"a bucranium is a cattle skull plastered with clay. It is most frequently part of the house inventory, placed inside the house or hung on the outer wall… According to the current evidence, at least 30 bucrania have been retrieved from Vinča culture settlements in Serbia." Cattle to settle – Bull to rule among Late Neolithic Vinča culture Miloš Spasić.

An early myth relates how, in the beginning, there was nothing but chaos in the form of unending waters. The Greeks have recorded our history, through mythology, depicting it within their art, because there was no other way to tell the story.

The Ancient Greek mythology tells us of the goddess Eurynome V-R-Y-NM has separated the water from the air and began her dance of creation with the serpent Ophion (FN).

Going back many thousands of years, sound and its frequencies, and sacred symbols, together with colors had expressed the full microcosms of biology, mathematics, chemistry and metaphysics of the philosophy of their time.

In Ancient Egypt, at the centre of Mediterranean, the macrocosmos reflecting in micro was seen as our souls pulsation with the rhythm of magic and HK (HX) was the name given to this magic = H as the frequency of Supreme God that expresses IT-SelF through every single individual soul or Ka. Ka / Ba, a female and a male aspect of our soul, they believed has many parts.

One of them is the physical body, the spiritual body, the name identity, the personality, the double, the heart, the shadow, the power, and the ⬚ḥ finally, that is the symbol used for the soul of the dead once it has completed the transition through the afterlife. How deep and complex the Theology of our ancients was, and how much we can all learn, exploring its secrets.

To our ancestors FiSH would have been a sacred animal given by Gods to all of the nations, so within various languages we find: RiBa (in Slavic), PeZ in Spanish, HuT in Arabic, all expressing the Gift from GoD. Our ancestors saw ReD as the sacred female colour so we got CRVeN (in Slavic), HoNG in Chinese, HaMRA in Arabic.

H aDaM and the Magic of Sound

Just about the same time, within Genesis or Old Testament, better known as the Old Bible we find the creation myth written as:

H aDaM

Following sacred H through the esoteric studies of our priests, and sacred books, reading it as the Sound of God, we get a beautiful undistorted translation of this phrase to be:

H has created D and M

H (as the name of God) creates:

1. D as the Male principle, the YanG of consciousness manifestation, creating sounds of D, TH, G, B or R (Dio, Theo, Bog, Beauty, Ben as Chinese for White, Brahma, God, or Ra) and

2. M as the Female, left, Yin manifestation of the Life force. M that is the first element, water, with the moon as its symbol, symbolically presented as the Eye of Horus in Ancient Egypt.

The Bible uses the word אָדָם (aDaM) in all of its senses: collectively as the mankind, (Genesis 1:27), gender non-specific as "man and woman" together as in Genesis 5:1-2, as for a male or in the collective sense, and the interplay between the individual "Adam" and the collective "humankind".

Within many different traditions, we hear our priests narrating the same story. We find the same symbols combined within the Ancient Chinese MinG that is the merge of Ri for Sun and Yue for Moon, meaning = Bright, or in the Ancient Egyptian creation myth within AmoN Ra.

The sacred secret Y has manifested as one of the 3 within the trinity of sounds (Ya-Ho-Wa), the sound D carried "da" as the concept of greatness in Chinese, or "tu" as earth, D as Pythagoras Do leading the music scale of sounds.

The sacred secret W manifested as the sacred M or N, K or L, P or Ph or as SH of death, or Č for čakra, or Čovek in Slavic, Č that has represented the snake, or the spiral or the Kundalini Force in Ancient Egypt. With the same vibration as Night, Meditation, MiNoS, Mum, Nirvana, Death, it is the YiN of creation. The eye of Horus itself, our sub consciousness or Karma, looking at us, always with the Goddess Isis as M of the Ancient Chinese, that is the eYe, but also a tree, or a mother or a horse.

D or R or B carries within its sound Ra, BoDy or BuDHa, Dio, the enlightened one. Bu in Chinese meaning "towards the divine", or a prophet, and a human being is symbolically represented as the cross + Yi (that is one) - + I (descending form heaven) to form a human soul represented as +.

For thousands of years this sacred script was used to record the history of the pharaohs, pass the mythology or history or help the dying to cast spells that help them in their after-life journey.

Learning from the Rosetta Stone

A starting point for understanding our ancestors ancient wisdom is that according to our ancient sages, the human is the meeting place of Heaven and Earth, for many represented as the number 10, symbolically depicted as the cross, +, and during the journey to the enlightenment going back towards God, or Theos...

Reading the demotic script, our oldest recorded script of the Golden rulers of the Mediterranean region, we read the name of Divine to be -

We find Ancient Egyptian name of God to be: NΘR (nTr)

NΘR = T̲ (within the Rosetta Stone) was translated in Ancient Greek as Theo or the symbol Θ. The true pronounciation was lost in time.

Na = to die, underworld, moon, a female sound

Ra = sun, light, FiRe, a male sound

The ancient Egyptians did not use vowels when they recorded information in writing. Phoenicians (Arabic script) also do not use vowels. With secret and sacred Ya-Ho-Wa we get the manifestation of 20 sounds and their frequencies.

When the Rosetta Stone was found archaeologists and linguists made a huge progress in understanding Ancient Egyptian writing. Written in three scripts this most amazing stone, that is now in the British Museum, was found in Egypt and to the amazement of all was carved when Macedonian Kings ruled with Egyptian Queens the land of Ancient Egypt.

The first script, you guess, was hieroglyphic which was the script used for important or religious documents. Ptolemaic Neo-Middle Egyptian hieroglyphic script, to be precise, if you wish to deepen you research. That is the top the stone. The second part of the stone is in demotic which is a script used at that time in Egypt. The third is in Koine Greek so that the priests, scientists and government officials of Egypt could read what it said.

Meditating on the language of our ancestors, we now know that the Rosetta Stone was carved in 196 BC. The way one reads the script is always starting from the middle as the most important symbol or sound moving its energy to the left and to the right. Following the ancient stories narrated with the sound frequency, given to us, researchers, through the Rosetta Stone, we get all sort of inspiring insights:

wab-sHm.t   Priestess

The name of Egypt = tells us the Ancient Egyptian Kings is WSIR, the Land of Osiris (W hidden from the exoteric use by the priests).

Osiris, god of the dead, or "diseased" since the belief was that the body dies leaving the soul to be re-born, in the after-life, that in his female form takes the name of ISIS.

The son of Geb, the Earth deity, and Nut, the sky goddess. His female form, Isis, is the goddess of motherhood, magic, healing, and rebirth.

wsir-pA-aan,   Osiris of Pan,

wsir-bX,   Osiris BaX,

wsir-skr   Sokar Osiris or Soko-R (in Slavic), the falcon male God of underworld,

wsir-HP   Θ(H)aPis Osiris, a sacred bull, an intermediary between living and Gods. Both Greek and Roman mention Apis, the sacred black calf with special markings, and the rejoicings throughout the country when a new Apis was found.

sA-wsir   the son of Osiris = son that carries A - Horus

ḥr.w   Also Horus

Hr-imn   Horus Amun (spelled in Ancient Greek as Θ ρ αιμον)

You get the gist! :) How misleading the translations were! One expressing concepts, other words at the time when the translation was done by Priests.

pr-aA Pharaoh

pr-aA.t a Female Pharaoh

Ancient Egyptian name of the Supreme God written as nH̱r or nṮr or nḎr symbolically represented as X, a spiral, a snake, a Kundalini moving wheel, the Supreme God

The sacred secret Y has manifested as one of the 3 within the trinity of sounds (Ya-Ho-Wa). Ya moved in its journey carrying male sounds, in Ancient China taking on the form of G (YanG) and in Ancient Egypt becoming a variety of sounds, R, D, B, G. D, D as Pythagoras Do leading the music scale of sounds.

Our ancestors were supreme masters in sound frequency, when they gave us symbols, or sounds, they did it for they had a complete science / theology within their mysticism and magic, in mind. Treat them as the most educated researchers of the Humanity History (the PhD holders, at the moment only 1% of our total population, those days perhaps 0.001%) who were trying to pass their knowledge to us.

The Ancient Egyptian PhD holders, at the time when this research came from Ancient China, or Tibet, or India, speak of the sounds that is used to change the energy from one to the other, so they call Gods; H̲ or D̲ or T̲ pronouncing them as TH, or Đ, or Č, allowing the soul to take the quality of the sound of Gods. For example the sounds R or B carry within its sound Ra, BoDy or BuDHa, Dio, the enlightened one. Bu in Chinese meaning towards the divine, Bu taking the sound of the name for the Soul in Ancient Egypt, or the number eight in China, infinity, meaning also a prophet, or a HuMan Being that strieves to become a God.

The ancient Egyptians did not use vowels when they recorded information in writing. Phoenicians (Arabic script) also do not use vowels. With secret and sacred Ya-Ho-Wa we get the manifestation of 20 sounds and their frequencies.

Sacred H, as eternal Tao manifested in the trinity of sounds that is symbolically represented as a Snake or a Spiral.

The sacred H from Ya-Ho-Wa, or as a sound that progresses in its journey towards enlightenment from Xs to Č to Đ and Š and Ž, depending of the Spiritual Path and its esot(h)eric or exot(h)eric nature, a Female or Male led mystical journey of a Soul towards a Spirit.

"In our wish to relate to omnipotent, omniscience, and omnipresence God, we use art, music or poetry to express since Ratio has no unobstructed pathways towards divine. The mysticism as a life-long research and devotion to God through beauty, is within each one of this structure. But it is not just beauty that surrounds them but their deep mystical connection to the sound, symbols and mini universes represented in each sound / word." Tree of Life, Nataša Pantović.

The Ancient Egyptian writing known as hieroglyphics, the sacred carvings found in the Egyptian tombs, are with us since 3000 BC, "medu netjer", the god's words, simplified so that they became burial texts, left within tombs of Egyptian Priests and Royalty as charms, or blessings to provide an after life protection, a writing system given to Egyptians by God Thoth.

With the knowledge that the ancient European / North African / Near Eastern citizen did not travel, except to Holy Land for a pilgrimage journey, the holy expedition reserved for Kings, or Priests, that wars were constant but totally local, the Danube region and the wider Mediterranean area, including Balkan was colonized, subordinated and subject to slave trading for much of the last two thousands years.

Todor Pešterski in his video Vedic History of Ancient Serbia, in a Roman Vila Gamzigrad in Zaječar in Serbia, shows a mozaic of a typical so called "Roman" Villa full of ancient Egyptian symbols, Ancient Greek Gods and Goddess worship temple structures, all hidden under the "historical farry-tale" of a Roman conquest of the area that was Barbaric and had no culture or art-works or civilization to relate to.

At the time of no travel, living as separate sovereign Kingdoms, Arabs, Greeks, Slavs, culturally, ethnically different, were mistakenly considered, first a Roman Empire, and than a part of the Austria - Hungarian or larger Turkish (Ottoman) Empire.

When in Ethiopia helping Sister Ludgarda within her 150 kids orphanage, wondering the streets of Addis, I've learned that Constantine the Great (272-337 AC) born in Nish (today's Serbia) was not the first King to introduce Christianity to his Empire, Constantinople, later Istanbul. Ethiopians have done it just a few years before him leaving the historians and two countries to fight for the right to be called First to this very day.

The earliest found gospels of John, found in Egypt, date back to this time.

In an ancient monastery in Northern Ethiopia archaeologists have discovered Biblical scripts carbon dated in Oxford to be around 400 AC. A Syrian monk apparently settled in Ethiopia in the year 494 bringing the scripts with him.

The texts were written in Geez, the ancient language predating Ethiopia's Amharic.

One of the official languages of the region was Greek for it was in Athens that we had a school and the tradition of writing manuscripts. Egyptian was at the time written in two scripts – using symbols and using script.

The very ancient scripts were read from right to left using only consonants to communicate a word, without the use of vowls.

The sounds and the writing were considered sacred, and as such reserved for priests, who have through centuries developed a clear distinction between esoteric vs exoteric practices.

The knowledge of sounds, and symbols was hidden from masses, yet heavily exploited by the few to gain power over our subconscious mind. This is the environment that followed us for 2,000 years.

Since the Humanity has entered the age of electricity, we had more or less 100 years of exploration of unfortunately always Latin translated works.

Going back to the original sources, back 2,000 years ago, only a few documents have circulated among the educated classes throughout our ancient history. The mean of expression that could not be censored was Art, Music and Paintings.

A Latin liturgical fragment, a translation from a Greek liturgy, from 4th century AC is one of the earliest known Christian fragments to be written in Latin, and the Library guide tells us it is an 'incredibly rare example of Christianity and the Bible becoming meaningful to ordinary people - not just priests and the elite'.

The Worship of SHa

Many consciousness researchers have rejoiced with the discovery of Dolmans, ancient mini temples found in huge numbers on a sacred mountain in Russia. Our ancestors must have taken their worship of stones quite seriously. Even today, many come to meditate, bring gifts, burn incent, offer food and flowers, or just touch the stones in order to receive their energy. Some even dig to find 'sacred' but portable artifacts to take home. These stone temple structures built by "Giants" are 3,000 BC and are thousands of mini temples found on this Russian mountain.

In the Caucasus mountains of Russia, archaeologists had a fiesta discovering and researching hundreds of megalithic monuments known as "dolmens" with the megalithic structures now dated to the same time of Maltese Megalithic Temples: 2000 to 4000 BC. These dolmens, megalithic stones, temples cover the Western side of the mountain Caucasus, in an area of approximately 12,000 square kilometres located on both sides of the mountain ridge 5 km from the Black Sea, near the city Gelenjik.

More than 3.000 megalithic monuments registered to date archaeologically fall within a 1,500 years span of building, dated to the same period of 24 Maltese Megalithic Temples, dated to a period from 2,000 BC to 3,500 BC. These Russian megaliths are equal to the great megaliths of Europe or Near East in terms of age, quality of architecture, building style and the mystery that surrounds its builders.

Built by "Giants" these mini worshiping temples, made of the large megalithic stones were curved to in some cases make a perfect circle. The floor plans of Dolmans are square, trapezoidal, rectangular and round. All of the dolmens are punctuated with the round portal in the center of the facade. In front of the facade is a court yard with an area where rituals undoubtedly took place.

Each worshiping complex is fenced by large stone walls, sometimes over a meter high, which enclose the court yard. It is in this area that Bronze and Iron Age pottery was found with human remains and bronze tools, silver, gold, and semi-precious stone ornaments that helped archaeologists date the structures.

Following the Russian river Volga, we find a number of Neolithic settlements dated back to the period of 5,800BC - 4,800 BC. The Algay site, the archaeologists tell us, is located in Low Povolzhye (PoVoŽJe). The pottery found on the site was made from silt that consists of two natural components: plant residue and shell fragments. This pottery was traded between 2 settlements: what is now known as Middle and Lower Povolzhye. 520 stone items were found at the site and the most common tool was the end-scrapers (113 samples). There is a large number of animal bones: saiga antelope, red deer and domesticated dog! Wow! Even at that time! Archeologists have identified that the items from the lower and upper levels at the Algay site are attributed to the same, Eshanskaya (Š-N-K-Y) culture, it is recognised that the site has existed for around one thousand years.

When travelling through Greece this summer, I have visited Mount Olympus that is the highest mountain peak in Greece. It was once considered as the home of the Greek Gods of the Hellenistic World. In classical mythology, it is Mount Athos in Greece where the Thracian giant battled Poseidon, God of the Sea. Still considered very sacred, this area today hosts Christian Orthodox Monasteries and the Greek Sacred Mount called Hilandar, run by Serbian and Greek monks, hosting Orthodox Christian Monks from all over the world, accessible only to the male spiritual seekers.

Just opposite, across the sea, a place I still have tosee, is the Mount Sinai (Arabic: طور سيناء , Hebrew: הר סיני), also known as Mount HoReB where Moses spoke to God, saw the burning bush, and received the Ten Commandments. Some of the ancient texts mentioned within the story, place this event to as far back as 1,400 BC or as early as 960 BC.

In the first few centuries following Jesus' death, a number of Christian hermit monks settled on the Mount Sinai and in the sixth century, Saint Catherine's Monastery was constructed enclosing the Chapel of the Burning Bush (also known as "Saint Helen's Chapel") ordered to be built by Empress Helena, mother of Constantine the Great, who was from today's Serbia (Niš) during his rain (272 AC – 337 AC).

This Mountain was always considered particularly sacred.

JaBaL Ideid, which Emmanuel Anati has excavated, dates back to 2350 – 2000 BC. was a major Palaeolithic cult centre, with the surrounding plateau covered with shrines, altars, stone circles, paved with over 40,000 rock engravings. Archaeological artefacts discovered at the top of it indicate that it was once covered by polished shiny blue slate, paved work of sapphire stone; used some 1,000s of years before the Roman era, very likely chosen so it reflects the moon-light. Scholars have since theorized that Sinai must have been the word for moon "s-n". My Ethiopian daughter's name is SiNTHaYu. The main centre of moon worship seems to have been in the south of this amazing mountain run by the priests or priestess that had built shrines, and have left many temples.

The Christians, the Arabs, the Hebrews, and the archaeologists do not quite agree of how the exact history of this place looked like, but 100s of years later. they all sent their worshippers to these mountains in Egypt or Jordan.

The Prophet Elo-Y-Sha has visited the mountain and has called it: the gathering place of the gods or the mountain of BaSHan.

The Mountain ShaRa in Egypt or Jordan, is the gathering place of Gods where Moses, according to Bible, has spoken to God, was the name given to the Sinai mountain by the Egyptians. The Hebrew Moshe, the prophet, teacher, and the leader who in the Covenant ceremony at Mt. Sinai, has received the Ten Commandments was from the tribe of Levi, one of the groups in Egypt called H-aPiRu, Hebrews. Trying to time this interesting story, we come across, I Kings 6:1 tell us that the Exodus from Egypt occurred 480 years before Solomon began building the Temple in Jerusalem.

Solomon, by the way means, Sun + Moon. The Bible tradition counts about 12 generations from Moses to Solomon, which would be around 480 years allowing 40 years for each generation. The archaeological evidence also takes us to around that time, approximately 1250 BC.

The Sha entrance is the main entrance to the amazing ancient city of Petra (now in southern Jordan), the Song of Deborah portrays God as having dwelt at Mount Sinai, the mountain range in the centre of Edom. The biblical description of a loud trumpet at Sinai fits the natural phenomena of the loud trumpeting sound caused by wind - the local Bedouins refer to the sound as the trumpet of God. The dramatic biblical descriptions of devouring fire on the summit is identical to the description of thunder, and lightning.

The place at time had a natural amphitheater; a nearby plateau on which the large numbers of Israelites could camp, and an ancient spring.

The Song of Deborah about MoShe

The Song of Deborah, which textual scholars consider to be one of the oldest parts of the bible, suggests that Yahweh dwelt at the Mount Sha-Ra. Today the site's name is PeTRA (connected to Christian Peter or Rock), DeBoRaH lived on the mountain that was considered holy, having been a sacred place dedicated to SHa.

In the Biblical account, God was accompanied by divine sounds coming from heaven, sound of female and male voices that have already been on this holy mountain.

In the classical rabbinical literature, "Mount Sinai" became synonymous with holiness, and the record tells us that the peaks "sang a chorus of praise to God", heard by El-aY-SHa, the prophet from the story of Moses (MoSHe) hearing:

"This is my name forever, the name you shall call me, from generation to generation." and has sent them "into the land of the Canaanites, Hittites, Amorites, Perizzites, Hivites and Jebusites – the land flowing with milk and honey.' Y or I am – H – W (vatra - fire) were the sounds given, as the vibrations of the Supreme.

Sacred Mountains and Ancient Worship

The ancient Inca also have situated their villages in the mountains, they felt these places acted as portal to the gods. In Japan, Mount Kōya-san is a home of 120 esoteric Buddhist temples. Approximately a million pilgrims visit Mount Kōya-san a year. It was founded by a wandering mystic, a saint, Kukai. Buddhists believe that Kobo Dashi is not dead, but will awake helping bring enlightenment to all people.

In Korea, people still worship mountain spirits, female deities, and one of their most important functions is to protect the dead. The Tibet's Mount Kailash is a sacred place to Buddhism, Jainism, Hinduism that yearly attracts thousands as the site of pilgrimages. According to some Hindu tradition, Mount Kailash is the home of the deity Shiva.

Shasta Mountain was worshipped by the Native American tribe, the Wintu, who see this land as a sacred graveyard of their ancestors. Shasta's glory couldn't pass unnoticed, so today different unorthodox religious practices happen at the tips of this mountain.

Saint SaBBaS / SaWa / SaVa about the Divine Liturgy

A Serbian greatest Saint, who was also a King (read: very educated), has left his Kingdom to set-up a Monastery in Hilandar, now Greece, to leave Mount Athos, this Holy Mount some 7 years later, to go back to his Kingdom building schools, churches, establishing art, to educate the people of Serbia.

If you are from Serbia, you will know him by the name of Saint Sava, or Sabbas is the ancient form of this masculine name, or Sawa (the name variation used in Warsaw, Poland) that tell us stories of how B (of Barbarians, the ones who worship "B" as BoG or GoD, have changed this B in to SH to be further changed into W, that at one point even hid the real name of Warsaw).

So, Saint Sava, or Sabbas the Sanctified, the Prince and the first Archbishop of Serbia has left the 11th Century Monastic liturgical manual, teaching monks how to pray for 6 hours daily, early mornings, live semi vegetarian life-style and eat fish only once a week (as Hindus would), pray with their hands up high, greeting God as Jews would, do bows every morning to greet the Lord (very similar ones to the Tibetan bows or Muslim morning prayers), uses these words to describe the Divine Liturgy: "Strašna i Božanstvena, Magična, Moćna" = Horrific, Magic, Powerful Divine Ritual.

The ancient texts would looked like the following Ancient Greek Prayer:

Ancient Greek Prayer ca 200 AC

Just observing the above, to all who are the researchers of the sacred sounds, it is clear that we ought to go back to the very original sources (Ancient Greek) and work backwards, de-coding it while adding the sounds that were hidden back in time...

Standard edition of the Greek text

The Lord's Prayer (in Greek) on an ancient Papyrus would look something like this ΠΑΤΕΡ ΗΜΩΝ Ο ΕΝ ΤΟΙΣ ΟΥΡΑΝΟΙΣ ΑΓΙΑΣΘΗΤΩ ΤΟ ΟΝΟΜΑ ΣΟΥ ΕΛΘΕΤΩ Η ΒΑΣΙΛΕΙΑ ΣΟΥ ΓΕΝΗΘΗΤΩ ΤΟ ΘΕΛΗΜΑ ΣΟΥ, ΩΣ ΕΝ ΟΥΡΑΝΩ ΚΑΙ ΕΠΙ ΤΗΣ ΓΗΣ ΤΟΝ ΑΡΤΟΝ ΗΜΩΝ ΤΟΝ ΕΠΙΟΥΣΙΟΝ ΔΟΣ ΗΜΙΝ ΣΗΜΕΡΟΝ ΚΑΙ ΑΦΕΣ ΗΜΙΝ ΤΑ ΟΦΕΙΛΗΜΑΤΑ ΗΜΩΝ, ΩΣ ΚΑΙ ΗΜΕΙΣ ΑΦΙΕΜΕΝ ΤΟΙΣ ΟΦΕΙΛΕΤΑΙΣ ΗΜΩΝ ΚΑΙ ΜΗ ΕΙΣΕΝΕΓΚΗΣ ΗΜΑΣ ΕΙΣ ΠΕΙΡΑΣΜΟΝ, ΑΛΛΑ ΡΥΣΑΙ ΗΜΑΣ ΑΠΟ ΤΟΥ ΠΟΝΗΡΟΥ. ΑΜΗΝ.

Отче наш, иже јеси на небесјех, да свјатитсја имја Твоје, да приидет царствије Твоје, да будет воља Твоја, јако на небеси и на земљи. Хљеб наш насушчниј дажд нам днес и остави нам долги нашја, јакоже и ми остављајем должником нашим. И не воведи нас во искушеније, но избави нас от лукаваго. Амин. A Slavic Version of the Lord's Prayer

The sacred SH, that later became W, in English, has changed its form into the Greek Σ, S of the Latin Spirito Santos, as early as within the translations of the script of the Ancient Greeks, hiding the SH vibration of Isis, the Death, the Underworld, Night, Meditation, MiNoS, Mum, Nirvana, Death, Subconsciousness, or the YiN of Consciousness that has in the Ancient Europe lost its potency with the loss of sounds such as Ž or Đ or Š or DŽ or Č.

There is no CH as in Cheese or as in ČoNo in Slavic languages, or Church in English, in the Greek language, so the first translation of any ancient text into the Ancient Greek Θ or ῶ. or Σ or M, got a different sound.

In transcribed Greek names, CH always sounds like K, the Ancient Greek also had a real K (letter Κ κ). At one point of our history, within the

Ancient Egyptian, Ancient Hebrew, Ancient Geez, all the names of Gods, influential people, Kings or Phaereos carried the sounds of Ž Đ Č, DŽ or SH, and all the sound rituals were conducted with this magic 111 Hz musical scale.

The Ancient Greek letter X (from Xristos) is later named "chi" (X χ), The chi is a hard H-like sound as in the English CHaoS, corresponding originally to Č + Y + S "ČaYoS" now pronounced as KaYoS.

Just a slight digression, recently, I had a unique opportunity to listen to the Mother Marry prayer in Arabic, for has been translated into this classical form of Arabic, spoken in Malta, fairly recently. We were together chanting Om Maria = Mother Maria, calling AllaH the Lord, so the chanting so mystically reflected this Universal knowledge of Sounds of Gods, AuM BaBa AuM.

Ὁ Λαὸς ψάλλει τό Κύριε, ἐλέησον

In peace, let us pray to the Lord

Λαός· Σοί, Κύριε.

Siii, KiRiJe (bless-me with S)

So why am I telling this to you? For, in the 2014 French science fiction action film written and directed by Luc Besson, the Professor Norman would tell Lucy: "You know... If you think about the very nature of life - I mean, on the very beginning, the development of the first cell divided into two cells - the sole purpose of life has been to pass on what was learned. There was no higher purpose. So if you're asking me what to do with all this knowledge you're accumulating, I say... Pass it on..."

So, I pass it on.

Passed through pictures, like the ancient Egyptian spirituality, whether

Christians, Muslims or Hindus, Taoist, Jews, Atheists or Buddhists, our scientists, applied psychologists and consciousness researchers, always followed their inner-most drive for goodness as their souls' quest, no matter what their have chosen as their personal growth system.

While in Malta I was graced to meet some of the most inspiring Catholic Priests, father George for example, helped my adoption journey introducing me to Sister's Luganda's Ethiopian orphanage, both of them around 60, still following the path of Jesus helping poor within their missions!

Back in the day, by around the 2000 BC to 700 BC, Mesopotamia was ruled by Amorites, the Amorites (/ˈæməˌraɪts/; Sumerian MAR.TU;

Egyptian Amar; Hebrew אמורי ʼĒmōrī; Ancient Greek: Ἀμορραῖοι) established Babylon as their largest city. The term Amurru in Sumerian texts refers to both them and to their principal deity. It was the largest city in the world (10 square km), the first city to reach a population above 200,000 people.

Back in the day, their ancient wisdom was passed to us, their ancestors, through pictures on the temples' walls or vases.

So, the whole world of mythological creatures was a gift of conscious and unconscious learnings and some exceptionally talented scientists of the last 200 years devoted their lives to translate these works.

When I for the first time held the 16th century book of Plato, in an attempt to closer examine the Old Greeks writings, I was completely intrigued by the book! It was TINY!!!! Since there was no printing press, his books were just a few A6 pages long.

So when we read "1,000s of Greek boats sailed across the sea to battle a monster…" we call it a myth, a mixture of truth and reality, yet ancient Greeks or Egyptians never drew an image of 1,000 boats, but two indicating "many", and they drew a monster not necessarily because they believed in monsters but perhaps to warn us against a more advanced enemy that uses fire as their weapon, or they encountered a disease sent by Gods – a type of madness perhaps for drinking salty waters, etc...

How deeply words get lost in translation!

If you wish to explore any ancient subject further, I encourage you, my dear consciousness researcher, to follow the original texts of our ancestors trusting their wisdom inspired logic, going back to the ancient Egyptian paintings and Greek paintings for the guideline. Trust me, our brains are no better nor worse than our ancestors', we just live surrounded by different set of circumstances, and we may or may not use the opportunity to learn from their wisdom inspired knowledge.

Apollo was the God of healing, music and poetry, but also of oracles. Is this a message to use poetry, and music while talking to Gods?

The Divine Liturgy by Justin the Martyr

The most ancient description of the order and time of the Divine Liturgy is written in 138 AC by Justin the Martyr, a Christian saint, a well studied man who in his Dialogue tells us of his early education, his theological and metaphysical inspiration coming from the philosophers of Stoic, Pythagorean and Plato schools. He refers to the day, as the day of the sun, the Lord's Day, the day of Kyrios, that is Kyriake, or Sunday, the first day of the week.

The lingua franca used during the Late Bronze Age in the area was Akkadian

Interestingly, one of the places that claims the holy relics of this Saint is the Jesuit's Church in Valletta, in Malta. Brought to Malta in the 15th century, with the remains of other Martyrs Saints, by the Knights, the Crusaiders.

Ancient Script of VinCHa

The archeological remains found on the Neolithic sites of the Vinča (Serbia) include a script that might have been with us 4,000+ years either as signs / symbols appearing or disappearing in the Mediterranean. Y M H X V W

Interesting for our research are the unique signs, indicating the Church or King's Property, usually identifying the owners: B or Delta or Cyrillic W (sound Sh). Some suggest a numbering system: 3, 9, 30, or 1 or the female energy that goes "forth" as 1. and some are the symbols for gods.

Foster (1984) observes the continuity of the Paleolithic signs for a female: "W", symbolically the same as Slavic Cyrillic Š and for a male = F = P(H) = PhaRaoH or the male energy that is represented by the 2 lines or through the action of "growth", or the number 2, representing a human being, the first number, since 1 is for God and it is an entity, omnipresent, omnipotent Divine.

These signs are significant in the Vinča sign system and occur frequently on the Lepenski Vir stone.

Using the above rules, we wish to have Θ or ὧ. or Σ or M replaced with the correct sounds.

The Greek Orthodox Christian Prayer starts with:

ἑνὸς Ἱερέως = 1 priest = the Slavic jenos = one; YeReSH-S, the Priest sings as: (H)YeReSH-S and a litteral translation of this phrase is: "H is Yeres (blasphemy in Slavic); so the one gives the ως "SH blessing from S = ISIS" = the holy man giving S / SH blessings to the auditorium" = Priest.

The esoteric sounds of Ya-Ho-Wa (Ša) materialises on Earth carrying the male and female sounds, in Ancient China taking the form of Tao through Chi manifesting as YiN and YaNG. This amazing Chi in Ancient Egypt became a variety of sounds of Ž, Đ. Š, Č, Ć, DŽ all represented by different sound frequency symbols of various Gods and Goddesses. In Europe this early obsession with the sound stays with the Pythagoras' research of mathematics, frequencies and sounds.

A Soul (DuŠa in Slavic) on Its Mystical Journey through Sounds and their Frequencies, is influenced by them, as the name of GoD, any religion will tell you, will influence your Mind.

The major philosophical question we face even today, is: can you kill for God?

Mo-She came back from Sacred Mount Sinai (the name suggests the followers of Moon Sacred Temple) with a straight forward NO, that has since been changed into many forms, and has been interpreted in many ways, on this most wonderful planet Earth.

Check how many forms we have today

Language	No
Afrikaans	Nee
Amharic	Aye
Arabic	Le
Armenian	Votch
Bosnian	Ne
Bulgarian	Ne
Cornish	Na
Croatian	Ne
Czech	Ne
Danish	Nej

Dutch	Nee
English	No
French	Non
German	Nein
Hindi	Nahi
Hungarian	Nem = Ne + M (SH)
Irish	Ní hea, nil
Italian	No
Japanese	Iie
Korean	A-nim-ni-da, A-ni-yo
Chinese	Bú shì
Norwegian	Nei
Polish	Nie = Ni + E
Welsh	NaGe = Na + Ge
Zulu	Cha

Most people do not realize that a simple 'yes' or 'no' question is not simple at all. The Finnish for example, do not generally use yes-no questions. Answering questions with a repetition of the verb in the question, is common not only to them but to many other World cultures. It is called "the echo response".

Latvians up until the 16th century didn't have a word for "yes" or "no", the modern day "jā" was borrowed from the German "ja" and first appeared in the 16th-century religious texts. As in Finnish, the main way to state "yes" or "no", is to echo the verb of the question, The Irish also use an echo response of the main verb used to ask the question.

Even Latin employs this ancient echo response.

Now, the original passed communication of Jesus, Ya-Shu was in Ancient Geez, Ancient Greek, Latin.

We, as scholars, have met the numerous translations of ancient texts in to a variety of languages. All the negations, could have been misinterpreted.

So the same Chinese Shi for Yes, or Sh for Sure, became a synonym for Sii of Spirits Santos, increasing the gap of mutual understanding of the basic "yes" and "no" between the East and the West.

So How did we communicate and JeSu, YeShu, the Son of God

JeSu, the Son of God has been translated in many ways, in an attempt to keep the original authenticity of the name and sound. Jesus (of Joanna of the Arc) has kept the strength of Dž and Xristos (of Christening) has kept the power of "X". The real sound of the name was Y-SH (Ja=Š or I=SH) as in YaSha and it has meant exactly that: "I am SH", the sound, at the time, worshiped as the name of the Supreme Female / Sun God by all the monotheistic nations of Europe – JeWs were the Ya-Sch followers.

Singing "H" of Hallelujah as the Supreme Mother Creation Ritual, singing to God using the sound of his or her name, invoking the powers to enlighten the people, was with the humanity during the time of Neolithic Europe.

The Arabic scholars were more exposed to the wisdom of the Old Testament from the less "Latin translated" texts, and were totally rigorous about the translations of any texts (had to be signed by 3 competent people and done in public) so they slightly disagreed, with some of the European teachings, telling us, the consciousness researchers, the story of Mo-She, Sinai Mountain, sacred "H" or hidden "Sh".

Nevertheless, you get the gist, JeSu was YaSch. I am Sh, or I am "X" for Xristos, as I am the Love Personified, or I am Son of Goddess SH, of Goddess X.

Within the wisdom of mystical teachings, this would be not R nor M, for R is a male manifestation of the energy that enlightens our science yet takes us into killings, nor M for M is our subconscious element of Mother Nature that needs the guideline so not to indulge in gluttony, drugs, medication or superstition gibberish. Not pure Logos either, for the Logos automatically follows the story of the Chosen Few that tolerate not LiFe and are always the first one to vote for DeaTH, weather death by guns or violence or alcohol or drugs indulgence, killing one-SelF for the SouL has no anChor in GoD or GoDDeSS or GooDNeSS.

Yet it is through the mystical Sh or X, that we seek enlightenment, it is the element that through love induces the higher states of consciousness, for the lady love tolerates not the FoRCeFuLL effort.

In our not so distant and in our very distant past we have followed Ra (Sun / GoD / BoG / Dio) or Ma (Moon / H / Sha / S).

When times were good, they loved each other, when times were rough they resorted to violence against each other. One would even hide the script from the ignorant so to stop them from killing each other.

The followers of the one God believed in trinity, the power above the Ra and Ma story, which has been called by many names, by different monotheistic religions.

Felix Romuliana Gamzigrad, Serbia

The village Gamzigrad, 200 AC, is at the banks of the Crni Timok River in Serbia. In 1984 the fragment made of limestone, with the inscription FELIX ROMULIANA, confirmed that Romula's villa was the memorial of Galerius, co-ruler of Diocletian and Constantine. Above the village at Magura hill around one kilometre from the main east gate of Romuliana, archaeologists have recently discovered an ancient grave yard from 300 AC, built on a sacred mound where burial and apotheosis of Galerius mother Romula and Galerius himself took place. So the palace, the temples, and sacred complex were, dedicated to Ancient Greek Gods, the emperor and his mother, and the post mortal Goddess Romula, who themselves became gods by the consecration act at the mount Magura.

Galerius worshiped Dio-NySuS and has deified his mother Romula and himself creating a temple and a ceremony to support this practice. At the time, an emporer can "qualify" to become "God" or a "Dio". Apparently it was a better practice, to first deify own mother, so that the divinity of the Emperor is passed by a blood-line.

"The mosaic representation of Dionysus and the wall relief depicting a sleeping Ariadne symbolize the idea of death – and resurrection, that is, they indicate the two acts of the apotheosis whose impressive material evidence was discovered" Maja Živić, Felix Romuliana – Gamzigrad, University of Archaeology, Belgrade, 2011

The floors of the rooms of the Palace and the Temples were paved with precious stone and under the floors the archaeologists found an elaborate system of channels used for heating the entire room. Underfloor Heating! At that time! Wow! The mosaics in the rooms resemble most closely the ones from the 2nd and 1st centuries BC, from the island of Delos.

"The Gamzigrad depiction of Dio-Nysus is the visual representation of this god's permanent aspiration to bring humans into the world of gods after making them immortal. Dionysus is the saviour of souls and the one who bestows eternal life. Like Dionysus and his mother Semele who joined the gods at the Mount Olympus after Dionysus' triumphal expedition to India, Galerius, the new Dionysus, and his mother Romula ascended to heaven from the top of Magura hill." Maja Živić, Felix Romuliana

Northern Temple

The temple is similar to the Jupiter temple at Dio-Cletian Palace in Split, built in 305 AD. The remains include a high podium, cross-shaped crypt, stairway and sacrificial altar. It was dedicated to the Goddess Libera

A belief in the triumph of Dionysus was the belief in the cyclical rebirth and.in the return to the Golden Age with Saturn as the divine power.

All the sculptures point to Dionysus / Galerius, and Romula, the ideological concept of the tetrarchy, being the alpha and omega. Jupiter is present at Gamzigrad, as the supreme god.

In the spring of 305, Diocletian proclaimed him Augustus in Nicomedia. On the same day, the 1st of May, Constantius who died a year later, was proclaimed Augustus while Galerius nephew Maximinus was nominated Caesares.

His principal residence before 299 was most likely in Sirmium. He claimed that he was Mars's son and Romulus's brother, and that he was begot, like Alexander the Great, by the god himself, who approached his mother Romula in the form of a dragon.

Historical sources tell us that in the winter of 302 AC Galerius stayed in Diocletian's palace in Nicomedia, to persuade him, under the influence of his mother, to stop the Christians conversions.

The entrance is ornamented with a luxurious mosaic with the image of the Greek god Dio-Nysus. Parts of a sculpture of Galerius depicted as Pantocrator (ruler of Universe) have been found throughout the buildings, a left hand holding a globe of red porphyry.

The other architectural elements are the relief ornaments symbolizing immortality: the picking of grapes, the intertwined vine. The mother, Diva Romula got the temple in the north part of the palace. There were other 2 females living in the estate, the wife Valeria and the daughter Maxi-Milla.

The Palace walls are covered with marble, green porphyry and frescoes. The marble sculptures depicting the Greek gods are made according to 5th and 4th century BC sculptural art.

In the very vicinity of the temple a great number of sculptures of white marble was found, with the most impressive heads of Jupiter and Hercules. The tradition was for the rulers to be named after Jupiter and Hercules and that the annual holiday is set up on the day when the augusti identified themselves with Jupiter and caesari with Hercules – the day which became their birthday (geminus natalis).

Ancient Balkan

The so called sacred topography of the Balkans, the northern frontier of the Roman Empire, from the banks of the Danube to the Adriatic Sea, to the south of the Peninsula towards Thessaloniki in Greece, and beyond, towards Malta, Cyprus, Egypt, is Ancient Europe

Dionysus was the Ancient Europe's saviour of souls and the one who bestows eternal life.

The striving for liberation of the Dionysian cult is at the core of Ancient Greek / Europe spirituality. It is from the Dionysian rites that the idea of the soul related to the divine and the soul immortality was passed to the Humankind.

According to some of our scientists and researchers, the first King Minos was the son of Zeus and Europa, the 'good' king Minos, recorded within our 1,000s of years old mythological records, read artistic visions, read subconscious wisdom, he was held in such esteem by the Olympian gods that, after he died, he was made one of the three 'Judges of the Dead'.

The Pyramid Texts, 2400 BC, suggest the nature of the pharaoh to be both Horus and Osiris. The pharaoh, as Horus in life, becomes Osiris in death, where s/he unites with the realm of gods. New incarnations of Horus are blessed as new pharaohs. Isis is an etheric mum of Pharaohs, while an incarnated divine soul of her son Horus is within their material form on Earth. This is the reason why many of the oldest-known Egyptian pharaohs were only known by the name of HoRuS. It is interesting that we later get the name of H-R-S-T-oS as HoRuS the son of ISiS.

She was the goddess, energy, spirit that makes a man into a king. She is the number 3 of the trinity, Her son Horus was an incarnate of each living pharaoh. This myth was reproduced all throughout the planet Earth, with the Kings being the re-incarnates of Gods.

The Greek and Egyptian culture were highly intermingled at this time, one could probably see the same rituals dedicated to Isis in Egyptian temples and in front of her statue inside Greek temples.

Today, the Mount Athos, is a sacred mountain in Greece that is an Eastern Orthodox Monks secluded peninsula, known as Hilandar, a home to 20 monasteries, most probably full of ancient temples' remains to Ancient Greek Gods.

Isis, mother of Horus, she was in charge of the mortals after death experiences, her image is linked to funerary practices and magical texts and temple rites of the pharaoh. Possessing healing powers, in art ,usually portrayed as a woman wearing a throne hieroglyph on her head.

In one myth, Isis creates a snake that bites Ra, and in an exchange for the cure, to extract the venom, Ra gives her the supreme secret of his true name - a sound that gives an ultimate power. She passes the name to Horus (H-R-Š), her son.

Incas in South America and Machu Pichu

A different tribe of Sun worshippers, calling themselves Incas, lived on the American side of the Atlantic ocean. Thousands kilometers away from the Egyptian AMoN Ra and ISiS, they called themselves AMauTaS, naming their King MaNCo within a city called CuYCo in PeRu.

This remarkable civilization which Spaniards found when conquering Peru, unlike the Ancient Egyptians or Greeks, did not leave any written documents wheather carved in stone or on clay, or drawn on papyrus or silk. The fragments of pottery found on Archeological sites, ruins of temples and palaces, materials obtained from graves, and the physical geography or anthropology of the region, speak of tales pre-Christian missionaries, priests and Jesuits entered the region.

Exploration, excavation and observation bring us just a step closer in our quest to form a puzzle called: Ancient Goddess Worship in the World.

One of Inca Kings, TUPaC YuOaNQui, "rich in all the virtues", had many children and was remembered as a wise ruler. Known as a friend with his neighbors, exchanging gifts, he taught his sons the art of government and wise counsellors.

His rule was not followed by comets, bad omens and earthquakes, he offered sacrifices to gods and has implemented rules in his kingdom. The legend of the AMauTaS speak of a sacred cave where the Incas originated from.

This cave offered sanctuaries to all the Royal refugees. TuPaC CauRi was the one to draft a law, that under the death punishment, no one should traffic in scripts on the parchments or leaves of trees, nor should use any sort of letters. At one point, a legend narrates, a learned MaMauTa invented some characters and was burnt alive.

The fear and the superstition of the priests stopped INCaS in developing own writing.

MaNCo CaPaC had brave and disciplined soldiers, and he was recognized as the most powerful chief. The rule of his dynasty was the rule of a benevolent despot. CuZCo was captured by the Spaniards in 1533. Peru with its millions of people, and its most amazing wealth fell into the hands of a few hundred Spanish soldiers. They appeared from north carrying weapons "which used thunder and lightening" to carry death at incredible distances. The Spanish conquistadors seam to manage to conquer mysterious and supernatural powers.

The Incas saluted their King saying; "Child of the Sun though art the child of the day" turning their faces and hands towards the rising Sun, chanting Ha or Ra or Sha or Si in the most natural and widespread ritual of ancient worlds worship.

The records tell us that Incas temples were full of "Chosen Women" trained by Priests in sewing, art, cooking, singing with the best ones given to the King's Court or creating garments for the community.

The House of Sun, the Temple, was home to TuPaC aMaRu, the 3rd son of the King,. He was brought up by the Chosen Women and happily married to one of them, when Philio II has decided to exterminate the Inca Royal family. Father Callancha's Chronicle gives a story of the slaughter of Incas which followed. The Spanish soldiers were commanded by a Captan Garcia, who had married a niece of Tupac Amoru. The captured Inca chiefs were tortured to death. Tupac Amaru's wife was killed before his eyes. His head was cut off and placed on a pole in the plaza.

Hunters for treasure, many a time, from many different countires, often commissioned by their Kings, have gathered their resources and have searched Egypt or Peru or ancient sites of Crete for gold.

In 1911, a different type of hunter, from the US University of Yale, called Hiram Bingham, with his group of scientific researchers, in an expedition has discovered a biggest ancient Peru's Inca city, now known as: Machu Pichu.

He recalls "Suddenly, without any warning, under a huge overhanging ledge the boy showed me a cave beautifully lined with the finest cut stone. It had evidently been a royal mausoleum. On top of this particular ledge was a semicircular building... The lower courses, of particularly large ashlars, gave it a look of solidity.

The upper courses, diminishing in size towards the top, lent grace and delicacy to the structure. The flowing lines, the symmetrical arraignment of the ashlars, and the gradual gradation of the courses, combined to produce a wonderful effect, softer and more pleasing than that of the marble temples of the Old World. Owing to the absence of mortar, there were no ugly spaces between the rocks. On account of the beauty of the white granite this structure surpassed in attractiveness the best Inca walls in Cuzco, which had caused visitors to marvel for four centuries. It seemed like an unbelievable dream.

Dimly, I began to realize that this wll and its adjoining semicircular temple over the cave were as fine as the finest stonework in the world. Surprise followed surprise in bewildering succession. Suddenly we found ourselves standing in front of the ruins of two of the finest and most interesting structures in ancient America. Made of beautiful white granite, the walls contained blocks of Cyclopean size, higher than a man. The sight held me spellbound. Each building had only three walls and was entirely open on one side. The principal temple had walls 12 feet high... "

Malta Temples

In Malta, for around 1,500 years, flourished a unique culture that has built stone temples using megalithic stones above and under the ground, worshiping Death, Mother Goddess, Creation and Dreams. The Temple Culture, the archeologists call it, has built more than 24 temples on a tiny island in the middle of Mediterranean. Their building masterwork has started 3,500 BC, bloomed for a long time, over 1,500 years, and has disappeared by 2,500 BC, around the time at which the pharaohs of Egypt begun building their pyramids.

There is a complete absence of evidence in any form for warfare, weapons, defensive sites, wounds on skeletons. All evidence indicate a stable, peaceful and artistic community.

The first Temples were excavated by Sir Themistocles Zammit. He has managed the excavation of the Hypogeum of Hal Saflieni, in 1910. He was an Archeologist, Director of the Valletta Museum, and Rector of the University, a very educated and passionate researcher who has for the first time entered these 5000 years old chambers. Exposing the sites by excavation, exposed them to the attack from the elements. Hidden for 1,000s of years, and made of megalithic stones, or carved in rocks, on my second visit to the Hypogeum, I have noticed that the deterioration has already taken all the red spirals that I had a privilege to see covering the ceiling of the Oracle Room just a few years earlier.

Now imagine this, the temples were covered by 50cm of silt, and soil, and a deeper layer uncovered the cremation pottery mixed with soil, rubble, dirt accumulated in 1000s of years. Each one of them and they were more than 24 at the space covering the Maltese Islands.

Carved in stone, under the Temples, these goddess worshiping chambers, were of the colossal proportions, Xaghara circle hides the second known Ancient Maltese underground temple, similar to the Hypogeum that is a magnificent 11 meters deep, ancient architectural miracle that has the sound perfectly resonating through its spaces, visually imitating the layout of the Temples above the ground.

During this time, they were a part of a network of a trade that has existed at the time among Mediterranean islands and the mainland. The archeological remains speak of Mycenaean sea faring traders, various Sicilian products, and North African, Egyptian trading travelers.

No metal have ever been found in the Temples of Malta during the Temple period yet the copper axes dated 2,500 BC were imported from other regions. Faience is a substance created by heating a sand and clay mixture from Greece, Egypt and Near East. Faience was used to make funeral urns, and beads and figurines found in Malta. It was copper that made them bright blue resembling Lapis Lazuli (a semi-precious stone). Malta had no metals. Copper, less hard than stone was useful for it could be sharpened, recycled, by melting down and recasting. Bronze was derived from copper and tin.

Many dolmens were also found on the islands. These are simple chambers, comparing them to Temples, consisting of a large flat capstone supported on both sides by bare rocks. For the lovers of measurements, the one in Wied Filep capstone is 3.8m x 1.6m, propped up on several largish blocks at a high of 1.5m.

The names left behind are MNaJDRa, Ggantija (Ðgantiya), XaghRa (SH-aa-Ra) Circle.

Death Rituals

"...death is an important interest, especially to an aging person. A categorical question is being put to him, and he is under an obligation to answer it. To this end he ought to have a myth about death, for reason shows him nothing but the dark pit into which he is descending. Myth, however, can conjure up other images for him, helpful and enriching pictures of life in the land of the dead. If he believes in them, or greats them with some measure of credence, he is being just as right or just as wrong as someone who does not believe in them. But while the man who despairs marches toward nothingness, the one who has placed his faith in the archetype follows the tracks of life and lives right into his death. Both, to be sure, remain in uncertainty, but the one lives against his instincts, the other with them." Jung (1959)

Answering the question why focus on death, Jung replies: "Not to have done so is a vital loss. For the question ... is the age-old heritage of humanity: an archetype, rich in secret life, which seeks to add itself to our own individual life in order to make it whole."

Older we get, more profound is our relationship with our psyche. Jung translates the Greek "pistis", the New Testament "faith" as "trust", emphasising the importance of developing the trust in the psyche, trusting the wisdom of the psyche's timings, using the dream work to develop a relationship with the Self. Tending dreams, and acting on their guidance, respecting intuitions and synchronicities, one gains confidence to face the death.

Tibetans have elaborated the "art" of dying well, within their ancient text: the Tibetan book of Living and Dying.

Back in time, when our ancestors' focus was Death, the cult of Ancient Egyptian Osiris passed to us the myth of the Egyptian Resurrection.

The 42 (forty two) sacred books of the Egyptians, were circulated among Kings and Priests, contained the essence of the Egyptian death ritual. The most famous text of The Egyptian Book of the Dead is the Papyrus of Ani, prepared for the priest Ani of Thebes in 1,250 BC, creating a funerary text specifically for Ani, providing instructions to help the soul face the Gods in the afterlife. This ancient Egyptian Old Testament was the guidebook to the next phase of existence..

Funerary texts in Egypt were at first inscribed on tomb walls. The Coffin Texts have developed into The Egyptian Book of the Dead.

The soul is led from the tomb by Anubis to stand in judgment before Osiris, Thoth, and the 42 Spirits.

The very famous "I have not commanded to kill," "I have not been contentious in affairs." "I have not stolen," "I have not slandered," "I have not caused pain," - were first used addressing the specific Spirits - or spiritual qualities and 42 sins within the heart were weighed for goodness hoping for heart as pure as gold.

In the texts, the name of the dead is proceeded by the name of Osiris. The chants chanted over the dead body, wished for Osiris to be reborn again within the soul of the dead.

4,000 years ago, worshiping death our ancestors have bargained with Gods for the place of immortals, have competed to become the Chosen Ones, the Kings or Rinpoches or Saints. At first, the Egyptian mummies were ritualistically surrounded with papyrus containing The Book of Dead, later, we find them with the ancient Greek stories of Odyssey, or after Christ, the mummies were wrapped in pages of the Old and New Testament.

Death Rituals in Temples 3,500 BC

One aspect of death was the disintegration of the various modes of existence.

- Mummification served to preserve and transform the physical body into its divine form

- Book of the Dead contained prayers recited so Soul does not linger but becomes one with Gods. The name of the dead was written in many places throughout the Book of the Dead with spells helping this afterlife journey

- the heart, included "Logos" and "Eros", was protected with mystical words, sounds, psalms

- the ka, or dead-man's spirit required offerings of food, water and incense,

- the ba depicted as a human-headed bird, that "goes forth by day"

- the shut, is the shadow of the King, the psychic aspect of the personality

If all the obstacles are past, and the various modes of existence transformed, the dead person would "earn" the life in the form of an akh, aX, a blessed (holy) spirit with magical powers dwelling among the gods.

Facing Ma'at, the dead person swore that he had not committed any sin, from a list of 42 that refers to the ancient Egyptian concepts of "goodness" - truthfulness, law, morality, and justice.

The wisdom is of course hidden within the magic book writen back in time, hidden, so no-initiates can access its secrets. If it is the first one, the first ever, then must have been passed from Gods to the Blessed Ones, wheather Kings or Priests.

Hellenistic Mathematicians and The Magic Book

The Magic Book we, explorers, seek is the book of numbers, for the magic and mystery of sounds and frequencies start with numbers.

Hellenistic mathematicians in the 500 BC, preferred using a system of numbers based on the alphabet. To indicate that a letter is a number, they used to place a horizontal line above the symbol.

The Tetractys or Decad (for it has 10 numbers and letters included) is both a mathematical idea and a metaphysical concept.

1 or 10 or 10 of each number, or 1,0000 (one of 10,000) a number and sound of supreme God.

If the Ancient Greek numerical system, had an alphabetic letters assigned to a number, we could get some most inspiring combinations, 241 as 200 + 40 + 1 would have been ΣMA or 666 is written as χξ☐ (600 + 60 + 6)

In ancient and medieval manuscripts, the numerals had a letter + overbars: α, β, γ assigned to them.

The first four numbers symbolize the musica universalis and the Cosmos:

1 = Unity or Monad, zero dimension (a point), supreme God that has not materialised as yet

2 = Dyad, one dimension (a line of two points)

3 = Triad, two dimensions, a plane defined by a triangle

4 = Kosmos (Tetrad), a tetrahedron defined by four points

The four rows add up to ten, which was unity of a higher order or the Dekad.

The Tetractys symbolizes the four elements: fire, air, water, and earth, combined together to form 10.

It was Attic numerals that were in use 700 BC, in the region now referred to as Attica, the city of Athens down to the Aegean Sea.

There is a trinity (3) three sets of 9 numerals from the Ionian alphabet, 24 letters + one that is used as the Supreme Omnipresent God sound plus numbers: 6 Vau, 90 Koppa, 900 Sanpi, the symbols whose sounds today we do not know, for they were hidden by the Priests as sacred.

Another special one was the eight number (8), again not a number but a frequency and a philosophical concept.

Greek letter names are acrophonic: the names of the letters α, β, γ, δ, are spelled with the respective letters: αλφα (alpha), βήτα (beta), γάμμα (gamma), δέλτα (delta) so Koppa, Vau and Sampi indicate K, V and S.

Ar**ch**imedes of Syracuse or Αρ**χ**ιμήδης 287 – 212 BC, was an Ancient Greek mathematician, physicist, engineer, inventor, and astronomer, and he is considered one of the greatest mathematician of all time, The first to calculate the accurate approximation of pi, he defined a magic spiral bearing his name, he hypotheses that the Earth revolves around the Sun on the circumference of a circle. Archimedes was killed by a Roman soldier, and his original work was "lost" for thousands of years.

Can you just imagine the complexity of this task, can you comprehend the advances in science, and the thought form, if the Syracusan king Gelo II, pays the Philosopher Archimedis Syracusani to execute this research and leave it written for the future scientists.

In order to do this, he had to estimate the size of the universe!

The work, also known in Latin as: "Archimedis Syracusani Arenarius & Dimensio Circuli", is eight pages long in translation, is the Humanity's first mathematical research paper. Archimedes presents his calculation done for the King, stating that the large numbers were given to him to execute this exciting task, to discover the amount to sand that can fit into the Universe. The Sand Reckoner (Greek: Ψαμμίτης, Psammites) is the name of this work.

Archimedes counts in groups of 10000 (myriad), e.g. 10,0000 instead of 100,000. Within his work he refers to:

1 as "not a number" - for at the time it represented the consciousness going forth to express itself. In the latine translations it has been translated as "the unit".

Since the Ancient Greek number system is based on the alphabet, symbolically, each Letter has a precise "meaning", "numeral frequency", or "philosophical concept". Archimede for example, speaks of 'one', 'two', 'three', but also of 'first', 'second', third,. for 20 he would use: 2 tens or 2 deka, etc.

His numbers indicate nouns like: monad, dyad, ennead, octad, decad (or decade).

Interestingly, it is wrong to think of an octad as a set of eight units. It is eight units grouped together as a single unit.

This system became the preferred system for Hellenistic mathematicians. Archimedes tells us about the numbers that have existed at the time he was commissioned to write his research paper.

"In fact the names of the numbers up to the name of ten-thousand happen to have been provided to us, and beyond the name of ten-thousand we ascertain a number of ten-thousands of units when we say, "even up to ten-thousand myriads." from Archimedes, The Sand Reckoner

Giving the full respect towards the element Earth that runs through our teens as the hormonal and chemical misbalance, or a specific disease that physically changes our brains at the age of 50 or 60 or 70, we acknowledge that thought and words are energy forms.

Within the basic crude that is our body, our water intake affects waves of "water" layers within us; our breathing is our treatment of "air" currents or nadis, and solidifying further, the products of the "earth" effect our physic, the flames of "fire" manifest as the life force we receive, or not from the Sun rays.

Activities such as music, painting, sports, reading, all, are "esoteric meditation and study", mentioned by the Indian Sage and Scholar Patanjali, as the two out of three spiritual growth methods of liberation from the negative Mind Chitta, the third one being: Service. The self-indulgent behavior patterns, obsession with food, mobiles, gossiping or hate, all waste our life-force.

Activities, such as meditation, use Willpower to detach from the thought-forms, or self-train us into every-day choosing of more inspiring mind-chitta or life-style.

In Ancient Greek the Christian Orthodox prayer uses: KiRYa Siii, that is

Letter by letter, Bless me Ra with Si (yes), a positive attitude towards life.

Subtler we become, according to Hindus, we enter the higher chakras, according to Christians, the union with the Soul is Spiritual Consciousness.

A-Vidya Patajali says is the prime cause of all obstructions. Ignorance or the lack of knowledge is the cause of our prisons, yet we are ALL born into it, we are all prisoners of instinct. It is the conscious choice to turn towards the Beauty, towards the Expansion, towards Art or the Light.

So What is Metempsychosis?

One of Pythagoras's main doctrines was metempsychosis, the belief in reincarnation, that all souls are immortal and that, after death, a soul is transferred into a new body. According to Porphyry, Pythagoras taught that the seven Muses were actually the seven planets singing together. 7 (seven) is the number of the Music Scale introduced by him.

When Pythagoras was asked why humans exist, he said, "to observe the heavens". He practiced divination and prophecy. he usually appears either in his white religious or priestly guise, or else as a lawgiver.

"The so-called Pythagoreans, who were the first to take up mathematics, not only advanced this subject, but saturated with it, they fancied that the principles of mathematics were the principles of all things." Aristotle, Metaphysics 350 BC

According to Aristotle, the Pythagoreans used mathematics for solely mystical reasons.

They believed that all things were made of numbers. The number one (the monad) represented the origin of all things and the number two (the dyad) represented matter. The number three, a triangle was the symbol of the god Apollo. The number four signified the four seasons and the four elements. They believed that odd numbers (1,3,5,7,9) were masculine and that even numbers (2,4,6,8) were feminine.

Ten was regarded as the "perfect number".

Pythagoras were the first to teach that the Earth was spherical, the first to divide the globe into five climatic zones,

Pythagorean communities existed in Magna Graecia, Phlius, and Thebes during the early 400 BC.

Aristotle tells us that the philosophy of Plato was heavily dependent on the teachings of the Pythagoreans. Plato's Republic is based on the "tightly organised community of like-minded thinkers" established by Pythagoras at Croton.

The earliest Greek natural philosophies believed that nature expressed itself in ideal forms and was represented by a type (εἶδος), which was mathematically calculated.

The oldest known Pythagorean Temple is the Porta Maggiore Basilica, a subterranean basilica which was built during the reign of the Roman emperor Nero as a secret place of worship for Pythagoreans. The basilica's apse is in the east and its atrium in the west out of respect for the rising sun.

The church has a narrow entrance leading to a small pool where the initiates used to purify themselves with a water baptism. The building is also designed according to Pythagorean numerology, with each table in the sanctuary providing seats for seven people.

Three aisles lead to a single altar, symbolizing the three parts of the soul merging with One, the unity of aPoLLo or aXeN.

The emperor Hadrian's Pantheon in Rome, depicted in the eighteenth-century painting by Giovanni Paolo Panini, was built according to Pythagorean teachings.

Johannes Kepler considered himself to be a Pythagorean. Kepler titled his book on the subject Harmonices Mundi (Harmonics of the World), after the Pythagorean teaching that had inspired him.

Isaac Newton firmly believed in the Pythagorean teaching of the mathematical harmony and order of the universe.

"The Sentences of SeXtus" is a Hellenistic Pythagorean text. The earliest mention of the Sentences is in the mid 300 AC. The work had become wrongly attributed to Pope Sixtus.

The Rules are by Quintus Sextius, who lived in the 100 BC. SeXtus appears to have been a Pythagorean. The text reads:

- The soul is illuminated by the recollection of deity
- Bear that which is necessary, as it is necessary
- Be not anxious to please the multitude
- Esteem nothing so precious, which a man may take from you
- Use lying like poison
- Nothing is so peculiar to wisdom as truth
- Wish that you may be able to benefit your enemies
- A wise intellect is the mirror of God

In 100 BC Neopythagoreanism was an attempt to re-introduce a mystical religious element into Hellenistic philosophy.

Pythagoras teaching holds that every soul is immortal and, upon death, enters into a new body, he is credited with the identification of the planet Venus, but what most interest me is his fascination with music frequency of Gods, Goddess, Logos, divine, consciousness.

No authentic writings of Pythagoras have survived.

He has influenced Plato, whose dialogues, especially his Timaeus, are our closest records of Pythagorean teachings. Pythagorean symbolism was used throughout early modern European esotericism.

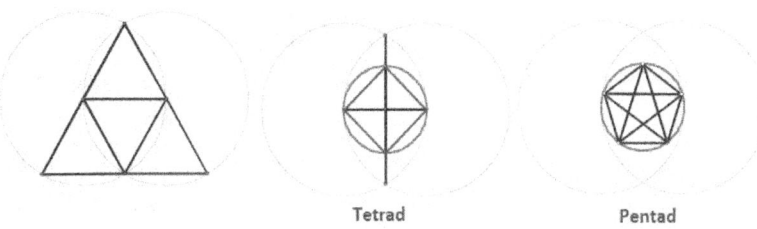

Tetrad　　　　　Pentad

Like many other important Greek thinkers, Pythagoras has studied in Egypt.

Apparently, Pythagoras learned to speak Egyptian from the Pharaoh Amasis II himself, and he studied with the Egyptian priests at Diospolis (in Thebes), and he was the only foreigner ever to be granted the privilege of taking part in the worship. Plutarch (46 – 120 AC) writes in his treatise On Isis and Osiris that, during his visit to Egypt, Pythagoras received instruction from the Egyptian priest Oenuphis of Heliopolis.

According to the Christian theologian Clement of Alexandria (150 – 215 AC), "Pythagoras was a disciple of Soches, an Egyptian archprophet, as well as Plato of Sechnuphis of Heliopolis." The Egyptians are reputed to have taught Pythagoras arithmetic and the Chaldeans to have taught him astronomy.

The Neoplatonists "sacred discourse" claim that Pythagoras had written the sacred text in the Doric Greek dialect, spoken by the Orphic priest Aglaophamus.

Pythagoras's teachings were definitely influenced by Orphism, they shared similar views on the soul and the teaching of metempsychosis.

While he was on Samos, Pythagoras founded a school known as the "semicircle". The school became so renowned that the brightest minds in all of Greece came to Samos to hear Pythagoras teach. Pythagoras himself dwelled in a secret cave, where he studied in private and occasionally held discourses with a few of his close friends.

Around 530 BC, when Pythagoras was around forty years old, he left Samos. He arrived to the Greek colony of Croton (today's Crotone, in Calabria) in what was then Magna Graecia. Later biographers tell fantastical stories of the effects of his eloquent speeches in leading the people of Croton to abandon their luxurious or corrupt way of life and devote themselves to the purer spiritual system of worship. According to Porphyry, Pythagoras married Theano, a lady of Crete and had a number of kids.

The images at the Ancient Egyptian Temple sites and Ancient Greek philosophers speak of SuN as the number 1 or Omnipresent and Omnipotent Goddess that as its rays emanates aNXs or "Holy Spirits" that enter the body during one's soul's journey through the earth.

Whilst accumulating experiences of goodness is the highest goal, reuniting with Divine, after the death, symbolically, one's astral becomes God.

Amarna 1350 BC New Kingdom is the time of AXoN.

The One that is Xa emanates 9 rays (aNXs) to the Left and 9 rays (aNXs) to the Rigth, towards the side where the King is sitterd and to the other side where the Queen is.

The two multiply into many, becoming three, for in their hands are the kids, and there are three (3) of them. One (1) that is not a number, but an entity, becomes two, that is a snake, a Kundalini force, a movement, a merge of Yin and Yang, and then three, a triangle of trinity forces that together symbolically form a DECAD (10) or 3 letters hidden within the Sun (YHW or YHSH or YHX) + 9 + 9 Gods or sounds of Gods and Goddesses, each carrying an energy form for "at the beginning there was a word / logos and the word was with God and the word / Logos was God"

The singing of hymns was the main ritual used for the celebration of the sun goddess aX or Sun God Ra.

The sun temples, were designed as the open-air platforms or with an open top for a better sun-rise, mid-day or sun-set views. Interestingly the female symbol "akh" or "anX" also evokes the Egyptian words of light.

At Amarna Kingdoms the Great Hymn to the aXen was the main Ritual offered to the Goddess.

The Great Hymn to the Axen / Aten / Athen / Atena is our principal source of this ritual. It is inscribed in thirteen (1 + 12))columns of hieroglyphs of the courtier aY at Amarna. The original hieroglyphic inscriptions suffered vandalism since their discovery. The following is the text published in 1976 by H.M. Stewart, of the Egyptian stelae, reliefs and paintings.

The Ancient Egyptians hymn is -

XaY.K nfr m Axt nt pt   itn anx SAa anx   iw.k wbn.ti m Axt   mH.n.k tA nb m nfrw.k iw.k an.ti wr.ti THn.ti qA.ti Hr-tp tA nb   stw t.k inH.sn tAw r r -a irt.n.k nb

The translation reads -

"You are Ra (sun), incarnated as Ra's Son. You bind them (for) your beloved son. You are distant, but your rays are on earth, you are in their sight, but your movements are hidden." Speech of the King, or Liturgy of the Priest, Babylon 2500 BC

All the frescos at ancient temples speak of the constant drive towards an omnipotent, omnipresent God or Goddess that governs all and is not accessible by words or art works. It is a sound but not a form, a concept but not a meaning.

The religious reforms of AXenaten, in the New Kingdom, were aimed at changing the monotheism towards the Female Goddess aXeNa, the story that was later in history referred to as "Amarna Heresy".

The Ankh

Ankh, loved and despised by many, have you ever wondered why... An ancient Egyptian symbol often drawn by our wise ancestors was the symbol used by priests and priestesses to represent reserection and the holy spirit. Often interpreted as the word for "life", it traveled across the sees to many ancient civilizations and as the sign was used in the artwork of the Minoan civilization in Crete (Ancient Greece).

The ankh continued to be used after the Christianization of Egypt during the 400 AD. The sign was used by early Christians as a monogram for Jesus.

The Minoans of ancient Greece in Crete, were one of the world's first great civilizations,. The Egyptians, across the sea had a rich, ancient culture that undoubtedly influenced all who encountered it.

Minoans were the first Europeans to use writing, their artists were supreme, and they traded widely with surrounding areas, building numerous palace complexes in the centre of each of their city states. Minoan society was largely matrilineal, and this woman worship was also a part of their religious practices. Worshiping goddess they did not use temples, instead, they had rituals in grottoes and caves.

Egyptian merchants (2500 BC) made written note of their exchanges with the Minoans, with details of the trades.

In Crete, too we find evidence of Egyptian influence. They share a belief in afterlife and, in the requirement of living a just life to attain life after death.

Even the writing that Minoans used resembles ancient Egyptian hieroglyphs.

The divine bull is at the centre of Minoan religion.

The ankh was taken from the Egypt and integrated into their own sacred rituals and burial rites.

Ankh or ANX is one of the most recognizable symbols from ancient Egypt, known as "cross of life", dating from 3,000 BC. The symbol is an Egyptian hieroglyph for "life" or "breath of life" = nh = ankh = nX

It is carried by the ancient Egyptian gods, goddesses in tomb paintings and worn by Egyptians as an amulet, a golden cross if you wish, around the neck.

The ankh symbolism of everlasting life or a symbol of eternal life, got easily assimilated into the early Christianity of the region.

The Egyptologist E.A. Wallis Budge (1857-1934 CE), claims it originated from the belt buckle of the goddess Isis, symbolizing fertility.

Deities such as Anubis or Isis, the goddess Ma'at, the god Osiris are often seen placing the ankh against the lips of the soul in the afterlife to awaken it to a life after death.

It was the cult of Osiris that was dominant as he was the god who had died and returned to life, thus bringing life to others. In time, Isis became the most popular goddess in Egypt and all the other gods were seen as mere aspects of this most powerful and all-encompassing deity. The cult of Isis promised eternal life through personal resurrection. In the same way that Isis had rescued her husband Osiris from death, she rescues those who placed their faith in her.

Hand mirrors were created in the shape of the ankh, the most famous being that found in the tomb of Tutankhamun 2,500 BC.

Mirrors were often used for divination purposes from the Middle Kingdom onwards.

The ankh was a popular amulet worn in life and carried to the grave. During the New Kingdom (1570-1069 BC), during the cult of the god Amun, the ankh became associated with him. The ankh was used in temple ceremonies and became associated with the cult of Amun and royalty.

During the Amarna Period (1353 - 1336 BC), Akh(X)enaten banned the cult of Amun and raised the goddess Athen (aXeN) as the mono-theist Goddess of Egypt, the ankh became her symbol. The symbol is seen in paintings at the end of the beams of light emanating from the solar disc of Aten.

The greatest ruler of the New Kingdom, Ramesses II (1279 - 1213 BC) employed the ankh in his inscriptions and it continued to be used throughout the remainder of Egypt's history.

The Ankh & Christianity

As Christianity gained in popularity the ankh continued to be in use. The Coptic church of Egypt inherited the ankh as a form of the Christian cross, symbolizing eternal life through Christ.

The ankh as a symbol of eternal life eventually lost its loop at the top to become the Christian cross.

Conscious Creativity and Transformation Tools

God created **Nature**
Full of **Chaos**
Where no two things are **Equal**
Where no sound, no colour,
no shape is repeated.
Man copied God and created
Symmetry, **Mathematics**,
Music, Straight Lines
Man copied God and created
Perfection.
Together Man-made perfect
elements create
an Absolute Disorder
Together God-made
imperfections result in an
Ultimate Harmony.

Perfection by **Nuit** Art of 4 Elements

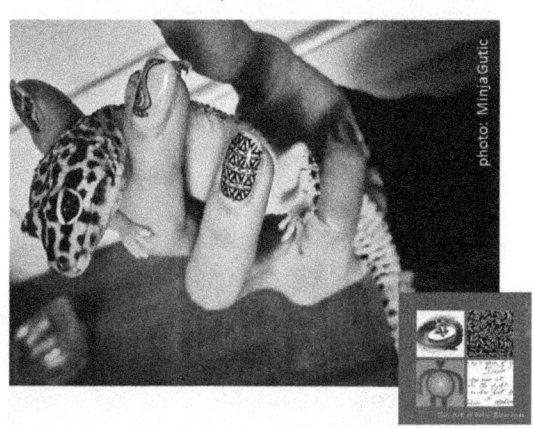

Conscious Living practicing Arts & Sports

Back in time, that has changed only a 150 years ago, pre-electricity, our society was infected with inequality, injustice, and a thought that lived within 90% of us for many millennia's - the thought of Equality. The total population of the world, post electricity, rose dramatically from 1/2 a billion to 7 billions. During this time of learning how to live together we went through both the 1st and the 2nd World War.

Thanks to our learnings and to the modern technology, we now have an opportunity to study / practice ancient spiritual growth / self development practices from around the world. This exposure to the mix of East and West, South and North, gives us some very inspiring insights.

A grand piano recital of one of the best world pianist Grigory Sokolov that was entitled "The Legend is Back" took us onto a 3 hours journey through Haydn's sonatas and finished with 5 encores at midnight. While on this "single man on a piano" marathon, we as his audience stopped breathing with every pause he performed. He mastered his and the energy of entire Conference Centre crowd, taking us into the highest states of consciousness.

Both music and sports, fully intuitively connect with the mastery of breath and souls' meditations. There are no exceptional artists, sportsmen or dancer without the mastery of deep breath, circular breath, rapid breath, or deep understanding of the magic of concentration.

Yoga and Tai Chi as products of Yin based minds

Yoga as a system of knowledge went into many details about how energies within our spines interact with the brain, involving drawings (mandalas), sounds (mantras), symbols (within each of 7 chakra). Yoga examines how the various physical, mental or emotional dirt within the body creates emotional blockages.

Mastering concentration, meditation or breath, brings both: prolonging life or attaining what Yogis call enlightenment. Yoga has developed some interesting "solder-like" practices for the improvement of Willpower. It was designed for mainly men and learned from the childhood. It comes from a predominantly Yin environment where the state of chaos is a norm, so it required discipline, as a male application of force. It assumed abstinence, the death of a practitioner came at the age of 39 anyway, so the time-span of temptations and the strength / ability of practice related to the amount of years of practice were very different.

Both Yoga and Tai Chi, coming from the East, products of Yin based minds, are meant to be practiced alone. Children because of their Yang nature are less attracted to these exercise systems.

Western Sports as products of Yang based Minds

The western sports were designed for our youngsters paying lots of attention to the competitiveness of our approach and the social aspect of the games, both a sign of predominantly Yang based minds. Applying the western sports to various age groups, we came across the regular nature walks, mountaineering, etc.

A tennis player has to play 6 hours straight within a tournament. If he does not have an inner strength and wisdom to perfect his/her breath there would be no possibility of success. Following the same knowledge, a Serbian top tennis player, Djoković, moved his diet into a vegetarian, gluten free one and later in his life into a raw vegan one, so he could gain benefits from the consumption of "live" foods. He comes from a Yang based culture, in today's world meat dominated diet, where the ancient Yin knowledge is intuitive and hidden within the practices of Monks, within long periods of Orthodox Christian fasts, or remembered as the natural vow of austerity practiced amongst the poor.

Why Spiritual Poetry?

Applying the Alchemy of Love wisdom within the sphere of spiritual Growth we acknowledge that yin and yang forces within Gaia play an important role of how we "tap" into humanity's for 1,000s of years executed patterns, do we do it with a "positive" charge or with a "negative" one.

Pure Logic and Wisdom Together in Unity, might help our journey.

Listening to our resonating souls we can either enter a spiral of negativity, medically called "depression" or enter into a contact with elements allowing Poetry, the Ocean or Gaia to heal us.

We intuitively use Poetry to Heal or express Joy!

Choosing to be alone is easier for a predominantly Yin based mind: a very young girl, a person that comes from a Yin based culture, like India or a Mediterranean country (a collective culture), or a Yin based profession - an artist, a doctor, a writer, a musician, physical worker, an old person, a sick person, in a Yin environment when it is raining or it is cold.

A predominantly Yang based mind: a boy in his youth, from a more Yang based culture (an individualistic cultures), like an Englishman or a Dutchman, from Yang based professions that requires lots of work with people like Managers, Lawyers, or Salesmen, would happily relax or "drawn" their sadness within a Bar full of stranger or with a group of friends playing football or wrestling in the middle of the street, in Yang environment where it is warm.

Gardening or Meditation walking next to the sea restores Balance

Within a society of predominately Yang minds, where Logic is a natural teacher, Humanity finds it more difficult to master languages. Stronger the Yang mind, stronger the difficulties to verbally express the thoughts. How many English-men living in England do you know that have completely mastered a foreign language?

Within a society of predominately Yin minds, where Wisdom is a natural teacher, Humanity finds it easier to master this skill.

The Chinese as a language carriers within its beauty, the positive learning expressions of Yin minds, and has embodied mysticism, symbolic thought, and philosophy within their most amazing symbols.

The Ancient Chinese used the Poetry of Symbols to express Life, Ideas, God.

The Chinese characters or symbols (and they have 1,000s of them) are an expression of concepts not words, so a simple translation of a set of symbols into a sentence might become a complete adventurous journey of deeply understanding the intuitive thought of the philosopher drawing the text. While studying Chinese characters in Cambridge, I asked a Chinese artist, a friend of mine, raised in Taiwan and educated in the US, why I cannot find a straight forward word for "beautiful" in Chinese.

What he answered, vibrates beautifully with the wisdom within this ancient culture, "beautiful" can be beautiful as a flower, or beautiful as a woman or beautiful as an art expression, why limit such an amazing feeling within a simplicity of a word.

Logic vs Wisdom or Yin and Yang Communication Choices

Our ancestors used to live much shorter, some 1,000s years ago, however our patterns are instilled within us as a natural ever-learning implant. A healthy person will see his kids grow to the age of marriage before dyeing at the age of 39. Not much time to experience anything but sheer play of hormones within our bodies. At around half of our naturally to be lived life, we get edgy to see our kids grow into healthy adults. So we marry! Those days we used to marry at the age of 15, these days we marry at the age of 30, slowly moving this line to 40. If we are at all married in our 20-s with the age of 40 we wish to experience it ALL.

When it hurts, listening to our always resonating souls we chose to heal either being alone or confiding in someone we trust.

If deeply hurt we acknowledge that we are hurt.

Being a heart specialist, my uncle who once told me that all heart doctors die from a weakness of their heart, has died at the age of 70 from a heart attack, and my aunt was experiencing deep sadness following this loss. Afraid for her health to relax her, my uncle's daughter, also a doctor specializing in sports medicine, gave her some sedatives. They have been teens left as orphans with 3 other siblings, at her age of 13 and his age of 10. At that tender age, for three years, they were sent to an orphanage together. At all our family gatherings I clearly remember them frequently crying and laughing together. At the age of 73, after being sedated for the second day she refused the medicine saying: "This pill does not allow me to mourn my brother. I do not want to take them any longer. My deep sadness needs recognition." So, she stayed crying for some months to follow...

Many Yogis / Taoist / Buddhists / Christian Saints use Poetry to Communicate with God / Divine / Life

"The Brahman's education began even in his mother's womb. During the period of gestation she was soothed by songs and chants in praise of continence, which in proportion as they won her pleased attention beneficially influenced her future offspring. After the child's birth and as he grew in years he was passed on from one preceptor to another, until he was old enough to become an auditor of the philosophers. These lived frugally, abstained from animal food and women, and in a grove outside the city spent their days in earnest discourse, communicating their knowledge to all who chose to listen. But in their presence the novice was not permitted to speak, or hawk, or spit, under the penalty of one day's banishment from their society. At the age of thirty-seven his student life ceased." from Indian Travels

Such was the ritual, and discipline needed described in Indian Travels, a manuscript written 2,000 years ago, to build a character of an Asian Yogi whose virtue and training equates the one of a Philosopher in Greece. Did you notice the life-expectancy note - at the age of 37 the life ceased...

Humanity / Gaia's Unconsciousness as Part of Family Lives

Gaia's environment is at all times either positively or negatively charged. Following the quantum physic logic, these states change randomly but in a typical cycle are distributed within the 50% - 50% ration (a side of a coin will have 50% chance of appearing once you flip it). This law greatly puzzled our ancestors and Chinese, for example, while researching this phenomenon have created Calendars mapping all sorts of "Heavenly" influences onto Human Behavior Patterns.

Building their wisdom system, using both Intuitive Mind (developed through the practice of meditation) as a highest potential of Yin states of Being and Reason as a highest potential of Yang states of Being, they have created the most amazing Calendars that listen to the heart-beat of Universe and the elements (within their system they are 5 in number). They have designed a diet whereby each item of food is related to the state of health called Macrobiotics; or within the relationship world they speak of the exchange of female and male energy called Tao of Love, and their ancient Confucius thought gave their children a strong drive for goodness.

Some 1,000s of years ago, to prevent the negative manifestation of Yin & Yang states of consciousness they built walls around their Kingdom - the Chinese Wall – that for some centuries stopped Mongolians from various invasions. Their Kings who were respected as divine Leaders were separated from masses (where they thought Chaos rained) within a secluded environment that only cultivated positive Yang forces of manifestation – philosophers, artists, the best of warriors, all ready to serve the King.

Yin and Yang Boomerang

Experimenting, applying the quantum physics laws to psychology, we assume that the Gaia's environment & human behavior patterns carry within the law of polarization of atoms, the positive attracts negative and vise-versa. Building a highly positive charge with no Yin manifestations of Consciousness, creates reverse effects.

Within China this state of Being resulted in a strong build-up of many superstitions.

Imagine this one!

Feng Shui was a science of determining where to bury the dead ancestors so the good luck will follow the descendants.

Priests, who were carriers of "Divine Wisdom" got so corrupted, competing for more money, giving the oppose advises, caused that people in their confusion stopped burring their dead, keeping them rotting in the back-yards, spreading disease until Government introduced measures to stop the ignorant from their stupidity.

Businessmen and "good men" at work stopped acting when the days were not "beneficial", causing the country's collapse during the non-auspicious days. Recently, during the 20th century, within all that commotion Religion was banned.

Now, Chinese worshiped all sorts of Gods, ancestors, spirits, their worship is so profound that no Government intervention could possible change the way people relate to Divine. However, it was the Mother "Logic" that China needed as an input to their wisdom system. So they chose Communism to help in their over-all development, implementing among billions the equality of women, free education, free health...

The hermaphrodite Universe of each country changes at all times, breathing, constantly evolving while Humanity's thoughts evolve.

Yin and Yang Balance at Home

While cooking we learned that a saucepan is easiest to clean when we have just cooked or when it is new. If the pot is already burnt, one needs to soak it for hours.

Most of us are aware of the same pattern within the mental and emotional sphere of human thoughts. We get worried seeing our kids aggressive, naturally fearing the aggression repeating in their adulthood. We get worried seeing our countries deteriorate with ignorant men or women.

None of us wishes our kids to grow within a disturbed environment.

None wishes to see kids lazy, attached to technology or lying, yet we see our little ones surrounded by modern "Influencers" endlessly shaping their little minds.

In our ignorance, starting a family, we believe that Kids fall from trees "perfect", or that their up-bringing makes the rebellious phase disappear.

The TRUTH is that the amount of work necessary to shape them into conscious human beings is HUGE!

These days, parents' aims are higher than a "survival", they fight for the kids' emotional, mental and physical betterment aiming for the highest.

Conscious Parenting observing Yin & Yang within Kids

Parenting kids, we are at all times challenged, within this matrix of Yin / Yang forces.

For example, a father with more Yang forces might act over-aggressively, once faced with a strong negative application of Yin or a strong negative application of Yang within his kids. Accepting this fact, men more-or-less left the early stage parenting in the hands of women, keeping the task of a Knight, safeguarding the environment, making the day-to-day decisions for the benefit of the whole family.

Animals act sub-consciously. A baby dog's behavior is a perfect example of totally Yang states of consciousness manifestations. It is advisable to have a dog before starting a family, for a baby dog or a baby cat will teach you much about the anger management techniques needed.

Both kids and animals respect the balance of Yin / Yang **forces** within each one of us.

When taking care of a baby Labrador while my friend, the owner, was abroad, I was amazed by the freezing instinct this dog had when meeting any baby human. A one year old baby has approached us, surprising all, putting her hands directly into the dog's jaw, before any of us grown-ups could react, yet the 6 weeks old baby Labrador did nothing to harm the baby, staying super careful within their encounter.

Needless to say that the Labrador was not yet trained. The story might have had a different ending with a wolf, yet personally, I had many peaceful and loving encounters with wolves when I knew they have already eaten.

In our house-hold my cat (that is always free to go wherever she wants) did eat our bird (always flying wherever she wanted), only because my kids unconsciously allowed the cat into the house before they fed her.

A naturally Yin girl with her imbedded aversion towards mathematics may make the father furious. If her mum has mastered this aspect of her-being (has developed the positive aspect of Yang – logic) she might become even worse in her "war" against her daughter's natural aversion.

The best is to give this task to a teacher, or a trainer, we as parents, get too emotionally involved while teaching or sport's coaching our kids...

Important learnings from Yin and Yang balance of Nature is that using any sort of force, the kids will just go into further revolt when teens.

Remembering our not such distant past, mathematics were reserved for the boys while the girls' schools kept their learnings within the area of music, cooking, languages, sawing, etc. Mastering chess, in her-own time, my girl became a Chess Champion of Malta.

A girl at school, Ema narrated, was drawing at all times. A music teacher told her to stop drawing during her class. The girl responded – "but this is my passion!" This intuitive logic resonated perfectly with the Yin nature of the teacher who also had to struggle to materialize her passion within her life.

Why is subconscious mind an Amoeba covered in Mold
The Humanity / Gaia's unconsciousness is unavoidable part of our family lives or Teenagers and Slowing Down

Within the Yin states of Consciousness "slowing-down" is our Guard from all sort of abuse (during the time of slavery) or over-work when cultivating the land or working within a service or product oriented businesses.

Subconsciously remembering the horrors of the English Industrial Age, slave-drivers, or using kids as labor, when the working day had 16 or 18 hours. In a natural environment, fishing or cultivating land, men slow-down in winter waiting for the land to rest, women slow down when they have kids, old people slow-down when sick. So nature takes care of our natural cycles.

Within the Yin and Yang states of Consciousness, there are positive and negative applications of both slowing-down and laziness.

Within the "Logic" dominated society, and "competition" driven environment, one can become accustomed to ignoring the signals from the body. We may be slowing-down because we intuitively feel a sickness coming our way. How many times have you taken your holidays and collapsed? Within Yang states of Consciousness, a male who is a Manager collapses as soon as on Holiday. The "Yang" based minds have more difficulty to sense their "intuitive" mechanism sending signs to "slow-down".

While exploring the negative manifestations of Yin state of Consciousness, we all know that the land that is not attended will not give fruits, that a house that is not maintained will collapse under elements, that a child that is abused will not have an inspiring adulthood, that if our garbage is not-collected we will experience the spread of diseases. Our "logical" part is afraid of this "chaos"!

A woman more intuitively feels the need for "slowing-down" and she can direct the man within this cycle. This is why when Yin meets Yang in Harmony, Balance follows their lives. When they have kids this Balance is disturbed, both when in a negatively charged environment, or with the inflow of a strong Yang (a boy) or a strong Yin (a girl) manifestation of unconscious behaviors within the Humankind.

"Within Gaia, this amazing breathing ever-changing hermaphrodite environment, that is on Her own sufficient, Life flourished. Within her ever-changing atmosphere resonance is supreme. We as human beings and souls materialized on Earth to experience various manifestations of Yin and Yang states of Consciousness inter-exchange with Gaia's environment." Nataša Pantović, Mindful Being Course

Walking this story, that has happened on the Full Moon in August, during the Festival of Knights, in the surrounding hills of Monastery Manasija in Serbia, we will explore the various manifestations of the states of consciousness, some geometrical figures and fairy-tales that whispered secrets within my soul.

The Ancient Greek Philosophers and Poets used mythology to pass the wisdom of many subconscious struggles, we as mortals experience, using the most gruesome story-telling tools to keep our memory alive. Fighting against a foggy existence of any words put together, we need a solid emotional platform to give us even a slightest chance to remember – this moment. Hence Zeus killing own Father or raping Virgins.

If subconscious mind is more powerful How to live consciously?

The subconscious mind is an integral part of the mind that modern psychologists acknowledge as an invisible layer of human consciousness. My research suggests a form of an amoeba rather than a layer, a hermaphrodite, morphed amoeba that in some of its manifestations is covered in mold.

I'll tell you in a minute why...

The subconscious mind patterns are programmed by repetition, soul-to-soul contacts and deep emotions. If the emotion is "fear" we run a risk of raising a child that will not properly develop Own-Self but stay in the shadows of the Parents' Will-Power, or a solder that stays overpowered with his King who consciously or subconsciously wishes him to stay mentally and emotionally weak, so he can kill for his King.

When East meets West within the same Research

While executing my humble research on Chinese writing characters, I came across some very inspiring findings passed to us "mortals" from Ancient Chinese philosophers. In their wisdom inspired Knowledge, they depicted the mind as both feelings and thoughts, flowing from one's heart and brain.

An inner smile, symbolically connected the two Eastern philosophies within me, when I found out: that if one (he by the definition in many cultures) is saying "I", he points at the tip of his nose, an Indian Guru Sivananda claims that the unit consciousness meets the Universal at the same point, within the So-ham meditation, that is: I am It .

Today while meditating on the shores of the Mediterranean Sea facing the East, I let sun and water as the most immanent physical sources of life, whisper secrets of the life of the unconscious.

God, Shiva, Zeus, Yahweh, the divine attributes of omnipotence inspired me this morning, using the tone of the voice of Tarantino's main black movie character Samuel L. Jackson, who I've seen acting within the Hateful Eight, a film released in 2015. Tarantino is an American director, who in the early 1990-s, as an independent filmmaker released Reservoir Dogs and who wrote the script for this film in three-and-a-half weeks, believe it or not...

The voice of this black man stirring a deep emotional effect within me, for the sound altered mirrored all the Cosmos or the collective unconsciousness that represents Blacks', Maoris', Aborigines', Slavs' or American Indians' struggle against this molded ameba of the subconsciousness of Humanity.

Mystical Knowledge vs Global Literacy Knowledge

At the time of Leonardo, the highest educated souls, who chose the scientific research as their profession, you could count by hand.

We often forget that during the Black Death in 1350, the World Population was near to 370 million. In 1600 Venice had a population of almost 200,000 so if 1% of this rich and influential city could read and write, we are talking about 20,000 lucky souls belonging to higher classes only with a capability of reading.

The historians keep reminding us that the global literacy has grown substantially only in the last 200 years.

The ambition of enlightening the population was a reform born from the Age of Enlightenment (after the likes of Bruno and da Vinci). Only 12% could read and write in 1800 AC, after the development of the Press, perhaps we had 0.1% around 1600 AC when we moved away from the Ancient Manuscripts hidden within Monasteries. However, this drive by scientists was short-lived, and quickly replaced with Religious Wars and further expanded list of Forbidden Books.

The World population according to the UN from 1800 to now, has exploded, went from 1 billion to 7 billion souls living on our little planet.

At the time, if you could read and write, you probably were from a rich self-educated family who can afford home-schooling or you have sent one of your finest boys to a School or a Monastery that offered some sort of education paying fortune to do so.

What about the 16th Century Cambridge?

So remember, while the earliest written communication dates back to 3,500 BC, attributed to Korea, China, Egypt, Ethiopia, Greece, literacy remained reserved for our Kings, and Priests...

The Cambridge website narrates a 16th century story of this crazy trend of so called "lay students" who pay to get educated in Cambridge, UK, when during the same century, two small houses needed to be reconstructed into a larger place, now known as Trinity Collage by King Henry VIII.

"The effect of the early academic and religious changes of the century can be seen in the physical appearance of the town: a great new College, Trinity, was founded by Henry VIII from the two small houses of King's Hall and Michael house... These new foundations were concerned with the education of men for the priesthood in the national church, but they, and Trinity especially, attracted **for the first time** large numbers of lay students.

These lay students, their servants, and the tailors, fencing-masters, tennis-court-keepers, riding-masters and the like, who came to profit from them, put very great pressure on living accommodation and food-supplies in the town and created serious problems of public order...

The changing character of the student body is reflected in the curriculum. Henry VIII had issued a series of injunctions to the University in 1536 suppressing the Faculty of Canon Law and forbidding the study of scholastic philosophy. The study of canon law declined, and the Greek and Latin classics, mathematics and Biblical studies now came to the fore."

To educate a person and lead it into any profession, within the modern educational systems of Europe, for example, it is compulsory to go to school for at least 11 years, until the age of 16 or 18.

We still get all confused when reading the statistics of a number of people who have finished Universities in the World. There is always an underlying question - what do you really mean by "the University" within such varied systems of education?

During the last 100 years, the European countries have more or less all introduced Free Education for all the levels of study within their

Primary, Secondary Schools, Colleges and Universities, while the UK and the US kept the education in both Private and Public hands.

Within all of the countries in the "developed worlds", within all the five continents, we now have more or less the same number of compulsory years to educate a child.

Within Africa there is no FREE education, so no Public money put into any schooling whatsoever, so all the years we within the "developed worlds" put into schooling just simply do not exist within Africa.

Now, where the "developed world" still gets confused is what has happened to the ex-socialist countries?

They saw education as one of the highest priorities within their Governing, so they introduced free Primary, free Secondary, and free Tertiary Education for all, within all of their countries.

The latest September 2018 released the data from the Institut de statistique de l'UNESCO (ISU), of 25+ years old population with their degrees, gives us a statistic of the World students who just finished either University, or have done their Masters or finalized their Phd, showing figures of 60% of graduates coming from the Russian Federation, while the US statistics still stays at 43.5% and the UK statistics are in the region of 32.4%!

Country or territory	Population 25 years and older (in thousands)	No Reading nor Writing Skills %	University + Masters + Phd %
Australia	16,594	0.0	40.3
Belarus	6,676	0.9	50.2
Belgium	8,133	4.3	32.5
Brazil	125,015	22.4	13.5
Bulgaria	5,421	0.0	24.6
Canada	24,243	0.0	47.7
China	870,905	6.6	8.8
Ethiopia	32,047	75.4	1.1
Finland	3,951	0.0	34.3
France	45,236	2.4	29.4
Germany	62,025	0.0	26.1
Greece	8,228	8.5	21.2
India	631,611	48.5	9.9
Ireland	3,181	2.1	34.4
Israel	4,624	4.4	47.0
Italy	45,867	4.7	14.4
Kuwait	2,758	5.7	41.7
Malta	306	1.1	16.8
Mexico	70,259	19.9	15.1
New Zealand	3,019	0.0	31.3
Republic of Korea	36,471	4.5	40.3
Russian Federation	100,531	0.6	60.1

Finland does not confuse us, since we talk about the richest of the countries in the world, but Korea with its 40.3% is impressive. This very expensive task of educating our youths is now bringing a strong educated work force from different parts of the planet. Yet, we have polarized our little Planet to a huge extend.

Polarizing North & South Map 2018 Data Wealth Distribution per Adult

While doing a brief management efficiency consultancy work in Nairobi for the Barclay's Bank, I had an opportunity to personally experience opening of the first Public Primary school in Kenia.

The demand for the school was so extraordinary that parents in their eagerness to enroll their kids blocked the entrances of the school, so the teachers could not freely pass. Also, the journalist reported the Kenyan Government was appealing to the Tanzania kids not to join this enthusiastic crowd because the school cannot possibly offer the education for Tanzanian kids too. Can you picture this?

A taxi driver was enlightening me narrating his story, his parents saved money all their life so that they can pay for his education, so he can become a Taxi driver – it simply had not occurred that you ought to be able to read and write, if you wish to pass a car driving exam!

When we get something for Free, as we in Europe have, we have huge difficulties understanding that this is not the norm within our little

Planet Earth.

Walking through the streets of Nairobi, and shopping from their markets, I felt safer there as a woman on my own travelling, than when I lived in Cambridge, UK, next to a home-less house.

When in Ethiopia, spending time in Addis Abeba while living in the Sister Ludgarda's orphanage, going through the legal procedures of adoption of my kids, I only used local transport and walked through the streets of Addis and was not once endangered in this very poor neighborhood.

Helping a Maltese Catholic Priest, Father George, build a school in Africa, I had a chance to learn that a cost of running a single school (food for kids included) for a year was insignificant, in the region of eur15,000 was donated by Crimsonwing Malta (later bought by KPMG UK), so my mind stayed puzzled of why each company in the world does not do the same, when it was so obvious that it is education bringing all out of poverty.

Visiting my local grosser in Malta, who has tried hard to introduce organics and has never ever cheated his customers, I saw him entrusting his business to a Guinean man, from West Africa, born in a town bordering with Senegal.

Trying to deeper understand his circumstances, I asked about the number of languages he speaks, and was shocked to learn he is fluent in French, English, Italian and Portuguese!!!

The slave trade came to the coastal region of Guinea with European traders in the 16th century. French is the official language of Guinea, and the main language in schools. France colonized it for it is rich in gold and diamonds, in the 1890s. France negotiated Guinea's boundaries in the late 19th century with the British for Sierra Leone, and the Portuguese for their Guinea colony. Guinea declared its independence from France during 1958. This was his country's starting point. This was his educational drive, to learn all the languages. His drive for goodness must be HUGE.

So, why does this matter today?

Art at the very top of educational hierarchy

Within this ever changing Universe, while exploring consciousness manifestations, we get overpowered by a constant bombardment of information, impulses and sensations.

Like faceless dolls we walk through a variety of life-events meeting people artificially without ever truly getting to know them. The true reason is our fear that someone will manipulate our drive for goodness that has happen so many times within the Human History.

Having experienced the drive for Goodness within own country, yet always being reminded of "us" and "them", of borders, of -isms, we find it difficult to comprehend that the drive for Goodness is Universal, that the knowledge belongs to all, that our subconscious fears towards strangers and unconscious mis-trust stay deeply within our behavior patterns and it is used as a type of a psychological manipulation that no conscious human being wishes to explore, live-in and call: "own Reality".

Our artists with their mystical knowledge break these borders.

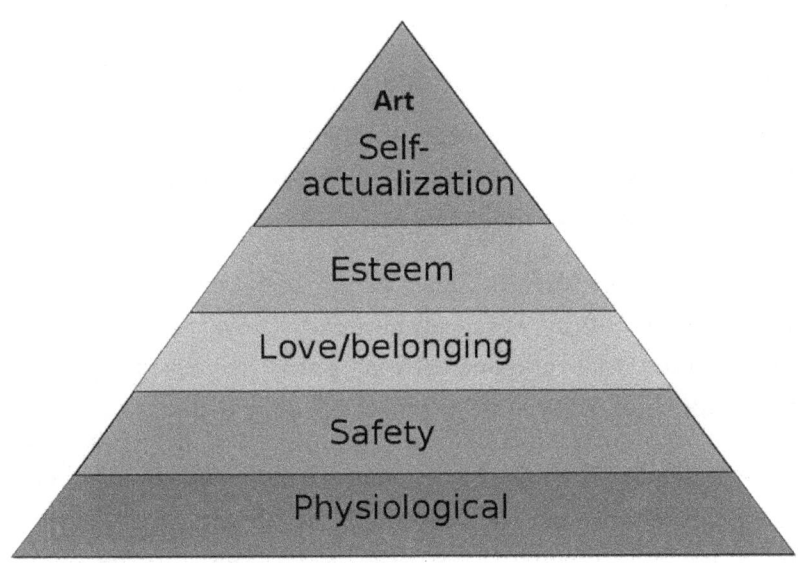

Art at the very top of the educational hierarchy

Acknowledging that we can start thinking Art only if our educational structure allows us to do so, we can start creating music only if we are given years and years of strenuous training, Phd research and writing books is far beyond the satisfaction of the basic needs.

Art, music, creativity are at the very top of the educational hierarchy and it takes years of training in all sort of disciplines for one to become a true artist.

"Music is a moral law. It gives soul to the universe, wings to the mind, flight to the imagination, and charm and gaiety to life and to everything"- Plato

Un-Conscious Mind and Religions

Kabbalists use blessings and curses while addressing this Grey Egg, to use an allegory of an Alchemist, a Hermetic Vase or Philosopher's Stone, shaped as an egg symbolizing creation, Hinduists work with tamas, rajas and satvic behavior patterns; claiming that it is possible to control

Kundalini, symbolically represented as a Snake, if and only if one is a Guru: the banisher of darkness that speaks THE TRUTH (sounds familiar?).

Christians and Muslims use devotion, believing anything else to be a black magic act leading eventually to misuse of powers in the exact same way Fascists have abused it, having an all "satvic" positive behavior patterns: instigating mass murders, killing for Goodness, regardless of the "Do Not Kill", the 1st ever principle we have learned as Humanity.

While exploring our concept of unconsciousness, Hinduists talk about belonging to a Karmic group, or belonging to a Casta, an elaborate matrix of supposedly reincarnated behavior patterns, packed in a system of thoughts that has tortured India for centuries. Within the same quest explaining types of human beings, an Astrologer talks about signs of Zodiac, or a Gestalt Psychologist explores a family or a Nation constellations.

"For indeed our consciousness does not create itself; it wells up from unknown depths. In childhood it awakens gradually, and all through life it wakes each morning out of the depths of sleep from an unconscious condition. It is like a child that is born daily out of the primordial womb of the unconscious. In fact, closer investigation reveals that it is not only influenced by the unconscious but continually emerges out of it in the form of numberless spontaneous ideas and sudden flashes of thought."

Jung, Psychology and Religion: East

This multi layered animal, resonates with instincts, security fears and habits while in the 1st Chakra, ruled by "safety" fears – with small kids and their parents this would be – a fear of dying of hunger. While transcending into higher states of being, within the Hindu philosophy moving from 1st to the 7th Chakra, as patterns deepen and we insist on virtues such as: physical, mental and emotional cleanliness., rhythm, devotion to beauty, gratefulness, compassion, honesty, goodness and conscious behaviour, we hope our little ones will stop manifesting unconsciousness in a form of rotten molded ameba, and become inspired conscious human beings.

"Everything subliminal holds within it the ever present possibility of being perceived and represented in consciousness. The unconscious is an irrepresentable totality of all subliminal psychic factors, a "total vision" in potentia. It constitutes the total disposition from which consciousness singles out tiny fragments from time to time."

Jung, Forward to Introduction to Zen Buddhism

Mystical Christians and Muslims, Tibetan Buddhists and Alchemists all claim with almost certainty that the only way to salvation is to pass the knowledge gained for the benefit of all. Christians and Muslims believe in the ultimate Christ's sacrifice for the benefit of All of the Humanity.

Alchemists symbolically represent this spiritual path towards enlightenment as a pelican feeding her baby birds with own blood represented in Ripley's scrolls as a dragon. On the other side of the world, Tibetan Buddhists devised an elaborative meditation practices where the practitioner takes the suffering of the rest of the Humanity as the Highest ever to spiritually experience goal.

Metamorphoses of Psyche Un-consciousness & Enlightenment

"Only by discovering alchemy have I clearly understood that the Unconscious is a process and that ego's rapports with the unconscious and his contents initiate an evolution, more precisely a real metamorphoses of the psyche..."

Jung quote about Alchemy

In our wish to relate to omnipotent, omniscience, and omnipresence God, we use art, music or poetry to express since Ratio has no unobstructed pathways towards divine.

The Mystical knowledge is gained through a life-long research and devotion to beauty, God, divine, through contemplating Universe or comprehending Air / Earth / Water / Sun as the most immanent physical sources of life.

These are different spiritual paths to enlightenment from the Himalayan monk meditating, through the fisherman out in the open sea, to the artist composing a masterpiece.

Forgetfulness and Unconsciousness

Until recently we couldn't quite understand our neighbors even if we tried...

The first Polyglot Bible was published around 1570 containing text in five languages: Hebrew, Syriac, Greek, Latin and Chaldean.

"For primitive man,..., His country is neither a geographical nor a political entity. It is that territory which contains his mythology, his religion, all his thinking and feeling in so far as he is unconscious of these functions. His fear is localized in certain places that are "not good." The spirits of the departed inhabit such and such a wood. That cave harbors devils who strangle any man who enters. In yonder mountain lives the great serpent; that hill is the grave of the legendary king; near this spring or rock or tree every woman becomes pregnant; that ford is guarded by snake-demons; this towering tree has a voice that can call certain people. Primitive man is unpsychological. Psychic happenings take place outside him in an objective way. Even the things he dreams about are real to him..."**Jung, Archaic Man, Civilization in Transition**

A German Philosopher Goethe, so much loved and appreciated by Jung, has done his first novel at the age of 20, and named it "The Sorrows of Young Werther" (1774). A literary celebrity by the age of 25, Goethe has written four novels; and treatises on botany, anatomy, and colour, he left more than 10,000 letters, and nearly 3,000 drawings.

The same constructive consciousness manifestation focused age happened to Nietzsche, who has also self-published all his work.

Tolstoy had a family fortune supporting his knowledge, so his wisdom and beauty of expression kept enlightening the Humankind even when he was very old.

Giordano Bruno, for example, has spent whole of his life researching and teaching Science as a Priest or Tesla pioneered the science of his and our time. Reading the works of these Saints, Researchers, Philosophers we do wonder can our intelligence even comprehend their depth.

While raring our knowledge perhaps we shall be planting a walnut tree, instead of searching for instant grass gratifications.

Trusting the local knowledge-build, with plenty time and space to express, choosing the best possible teachers, preferably poets as suggested by Jung, appreciating the wisdom of our ancestors, within this versatile Humanity, might help us enter the path of quantum Physics, Applied Psychology and deeper emotional comprehending of Ancient Philosophies.

Story of Isaac and Bartolomeo's Aurora

Exercising local Knowledge is like inputting various little known parameters into any picture, combining Gaia's wellness, health and pleasure, within a matrix of each and every one of us. The humanity's basket of experiences is so complexly bound together. We can see a spiral in all our progress including history.

When in my 30s I hated the story of Isaac, the son of Abraham and Sarah and Abraham's willingness to follow God's command to sacrifice Isaac as his new born baby boy; such a horrible myth where God establishes a relationship with Abraham through the sacrifice of his son!!!

Much later, I learned that we all do hate it, because no intelligent human being will ever rationally debate killing of own-son for any God's sake. It is a twisted mythological story of the Old Testament so that a natural parent's hatred will burn in our hearts with a justified anger towards even a thought form that supports such sick thinking, with a strong drive to detest it, "remove it", collectively attack it.

Light as Symbol of Divine

In art, the light is used to symbolically represent the wisdom within this versatile for ever changing Universe, so Christian Saints or Angels have light above their heads. In common with both the other surviving early papyri of John's Gospel; P45. The manuscript contains, consistently, the use of Nomina Sacra.

The initial system of nomina sacra apparently consisted of just four or five words, called nomina divina: the Greek words for Jesus, Christ, Lord, God, and possibly Spirit.

Use of Nomina Sacra in the Orthodox Christian art, the opening verses of Revelation - Ἰησοῦς Χριστός (Jesus Christ) as IC XC.

In movies, the light is used within films, like in the film Titanic, to increase the emotional intensity within audience when they are hearing of the old lady's splendid past. When watching the film, do notice how her eyes always shine, leaving us with this collective trust that she must be sincere.

Within the Humanity's past we met these inspired eyes when Philosophers preached, or when artists expressed their love for God, but also when we listened to some inspired youths with their "Holy Spirit" blessed TV personality.

"... even the angels thought Adam the lord of all, and they were about to salute him with "Holy, holy, holy, is the Lord of hosts," when God caused sleep to fall upon him, and then the angels knew that he was but a human being. The purpose of the sleep that enfolded Adam was to give him a wife, so that the human race might develop, and all creatures recognize the difference between God and man."

A Hebrew story, About family, a Priest explaining Old Testament

The History of Written Expression

Throughout the history of ancient Rome, the Greek was spoken by the well-educated elite. Within the Byzantine Empire, the Greek was never replaced by Latin - also known as Romanic languages.

China led the books printing revolution. The first completed printed book on paper is the Diamond Sutra (in the British Library) of 868 AC, during the ninth century. By the tenth century, 400,000 copies of the same sutras and pictures were printed, and some other Confucian classics were in print.

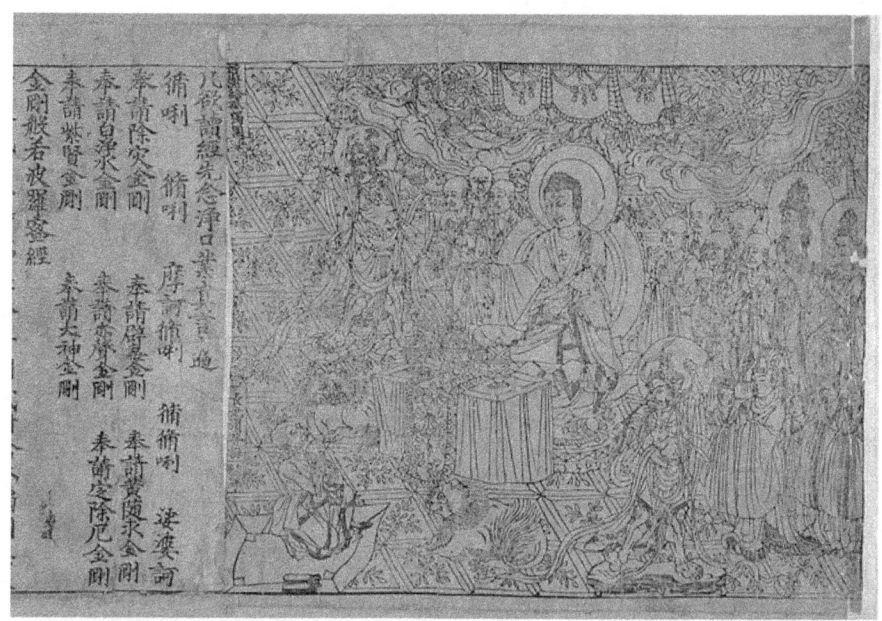

A page from the Diamond Sutra, 868 AC, British Library, London

Around 1040, the first known movable type porcelain printing press was created in China by Bi Sheng. Copper movable type printing originated in China at the beginning of the 12th century. It was used in large-scale printing of paper money issued by the Northern Song dynasty.

Around 1230, Koreans invented a metal type movable printing using bronze. The Korean form of metal movable type was described by the French scholar Henri-Jean Martin as "extremely similar to Gutenberg's"

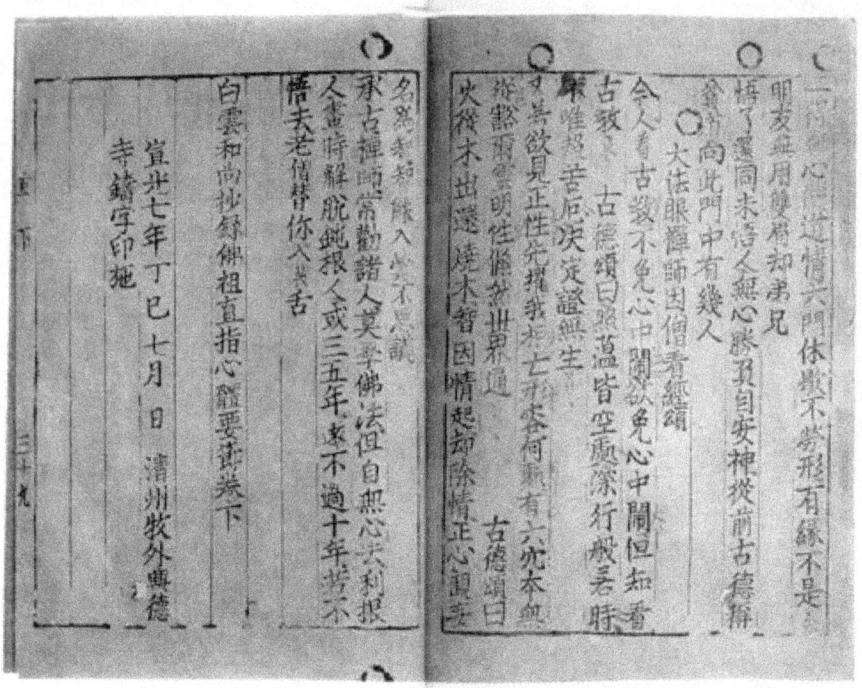

Selected Teachings of Buddhist Sages and Seon Masters - 1377 AC, Korean book, Bibliotheque Nationale de France

Christian Monasteries of the Western Roman Empire carried on with the Latin writing tradition. Before the adoption of the printing press, books were copied by hand, expensive and rare.

At the end of the Middle Ages, the papal library in Avignon and Paris library of the Sorbonne held only **around 2,000 books**, smaller monasteries had only a few dozen books.

The scriptorium of the monastery was usually over the chapter house where artificial lights were forbidden done only in day-light by enthusiastic students, priests and researchers...

	Proto-Canaanite	Early Phoenician	Greek		Proto-Canaanite	Early Phoenician	Greek
ʼ	〜	⋖	A	l	৭	⌒	Λ
b	⊓	⋗	B	m	∿∿∿	⋎⋎	M
g	⌐	∧	Γ	n	⌐	⋎	N
d	⋈	◁	Δ	s		≢	Ξ
h	🯅	⇌	E	ʻ	⌒	○	O
w	⚲	Υ	Y	p		⊃	Π
z	=	I	Z	ṣ	⟊	⋔	Μ
ḥ	Ⅲ	⊟	H	q	8	φ	⚲
ṭ		⊗	Θ	r	⌂	◁	P
y	⌐	⋀	I	š	⌣	W	Σ
k	⨆	⋋	K	t	✝	×	T

Canannite languages: An Official Ancient Greek Alphabet Charts

The history of printing in Europe from 500 AC to 1800 follows an interesting line.

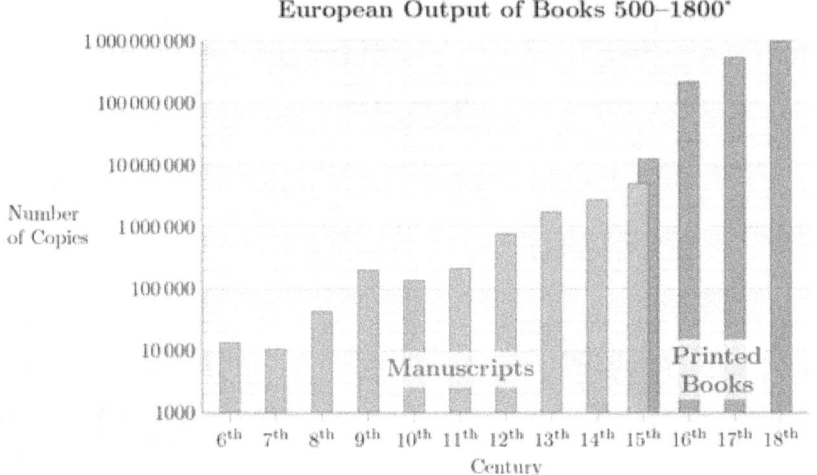

European output of manuscripts vs. printed books 500 AC - 1800 AC

In mid-20th century, European book production has risen to over 200,000 titles per year. Throughout the 20th century, libraries have faced an ever-increasing rate of publishing, sometimes called an information explosion.

Do you ever wonder within this explosion, what is your truth?

Burning Books and Forbidden Books

According to Elaine Pagels: "In 367 AC, Athanasius, a bishop of Alexandria... issued an Easter letter in which he demanded that Egyptian monks destroy all such unacceptable writings, except for those he specifically listed as 'acceptable' even 'canonical', a list that constitutes the present 'New Testament'"

When the burning is widespread and systematic, the destruction of books and media can be a component of cultural genocide.

We all with pain remember the burning of the Library of Alexandria (c. 49 AC), the destruction of Aztec codices by Itzcoatl in 1430s, and the burning of Maya's indigenous American civilizations manuscripts on the order of bishop Diego de Landa in 1562 AC.

"In 1244, as an outcome of the Disputation of Paris, twenty-four carriage loads of Talmuds and other Jewish religious manuscripts were set on fire in the streets of Paris." a Wikipedia source.

The List of Forbidden Books

We still find the lists of forbidden books by Inquisition within the archives of Vatican. This section can be also called - my recommended books of wisdom:

Banned Name   Works

Complete works 1585 Dante Alighieri

Complete works 1600 Bruno, Giordano

Complete works 1616 to 1835 Nicolaus Copernicus

Complete works to 1835 Johannes Kepler

1663 Descartes, René Meditations (1641); Les passions de l'âme (1649); Opera philosophica

1679, 1690 Spinoza, Baruch, Tractatus Theologico-Politicus (1677); Opera posthuma

1827 Kant, Immanuel, Critique of Pure Reason (1781)

1841 Balzac, Honoré de Omnes fabulae amatoriae

1894 Zola, Émile, Opera omnia

1948 Sartre, Jean-Paul

until 1959 Victor Hugo, Notre Dame de Paris (1831); Les Misérables (1862)

A Subjective Truth

When discussing the Lady Truth, we acknowledge that it always connects to our subjective Soul's view of the world. The truth means "my Objective experience of Reality", so with this in mind, do you know why Germans have the best bread on Gaia and why does this matter?

If you are born German you might even ignore a need to debate this little so subjective truth, agreeing with a Reason powered with Intuitive Knowledge of a traveler who explored 50+ countries on all the continents and is Gaia conscious. Yours ancestors' 100s of years of baking research that has gradually improved a super unhealthy white bread into a super tasty healthy loaf is within your set of local knowledge and experiences. If you are in your 20s, you will see no value in this statement. If you are anywhere over 40, you will resonate with it, because your health research has already convinced you of how difficult it is to get rid of an unhealthy piece of bread, whilst getting rid of Gluten, claims Djoković, the World's Champion, got him his first Golden Medal in tennis, while becoming Raw Vegan got him his last one.

When public libraries appeared, up to the 18th century, books were often chained to a bookshelf or a desk to prevent theft. As you can imagine it was not book lovers who would ever steal, for how many book lovers were poor or uneducated?

Jews didn't quite have public libraries where a "stranger" could possibly hope to learn Hebrew and explore the script within their local knowledge set-up. Judaism values the Torah scroll to such an extent that if placed in a synagogue it must be written by hand on parchment so a printed book would just not do.

In the Islamic Golden Age, 8th century to 13th, Islamic calligraphy, miniatures and book-binding flourished, yet none of the images within the books had any religious connotations. Yaqubi 9th century, says that in his time Baghdad had over a hundred booksellers. Today we find the most beautiful poems exploring God – Allah, yet the illustrations are very generic: flowers, or simple decorations. Within Islam we find no images of Christ or Allah, so no idol worship could take place.

Listening to our historians, we know for certain that the destroyed books, and art works are irreplaceable, often changing history in various ways.

If you are a Head of your-own Pack whether living in a Forest of Amazonia or fishing through Oceans, you try hard to understand the World the best you can. It is not always easy for all the followers of the Pack to understand that Life is a complex venture, always demanding new learnings.

Being too busy arguing various points of views, philosophizing, or fighting own partner, we assume that somewhere else animals do not need rearing, plants watering, sick do not need care, and children fall perfect from the sky. Within this life-long quest, so many of us create our-own little Universes, marrying and building own "perfect" families, yet the reflection inside the life-mirror says over and over that we err, especially when expressing judgments too hasty.

Respecting the knowledge of our Ancestors, Saints and Scientists, applying Clear Reason and Intuitive Wisdom within this dynamic orphic, hermaphrodite Universe of Unconscious mind Manifestations, at this stage of our evolution, we again ask own Souls how to live life healthier, happier, or stronger?

Ancient Alchemy George Ripley's Scrolls 15th Century

At the top of the Ripley's Scrolls, a large, robed, bearded figure greets the researchers wishing to enter this magic dance of words and drawings.

Identified as an Egyptian God of Healing Thoth or Hermes Trismegistus (thrice-greatest), the legendary figure of Alchemists, is the first one we meet holding an egg-shaped vase and observing seven alchemy processes, used in transformation of metals into gold.

George Ripley was a sovereign in Yorkshire living from 1415 to 1495, a Poet, Alchemist and Author of The Compound of Alchemy.

The Alchemist George Ripley was in a pursuit of the Philosophers' Stone.

Satisfying yours forever thirsty curiosity, this story travels through the channels of Cam, ascends the hills of Edinburgh and enters Oxford's castles, exploring very rare Ripley's Alchemical manuscripts that use both verses and images to portray ancient esoteric teachings.

For all the mystical researchers, apparently there are only 21 in total, 16 of these alchemical manuscripts are in the UK; inside the Libraries in London, Oxford and Cambridge.

Four of these precious artifacts are in the US bought from London.

For the visual lovers, the Ripley's scrolls we find today, are sized around 5m x 55cm, made of smaller squares, often printed and compiled much later than their originals, sometimes as late as 1800s, based on someone's trusted memory and detailed description. The smallest Scroll measures 1.25m × 14cm, while the largest is in Cambridge, Fitzwilliam Museum, and it extends to 5.5m×60cm.

They are for the first time printed in Germany, in the eighteenth century, with text in Latin phrases, they contain poetry verses and images of the process involved in acquisition of the Philosophers' Stone.

Dozens of alchemical drawings accompany Ripley's poems "Verses upon the Elixir", "Boast of Mercury", "Mystery of Alchemists", "Liber Patris Sapientiae", "Exposition", "Wind and Water", "Richard Carpenter's work", "Trinity".

For today's researchers, it is images that pass the message of our hermaphrodite Universe, of Kundalini awakening, of Life going forth seeking to materialize in all possible forms, of the sacred movement towards perfection.

Meditating on the images entering a journey of encountering various mythological creatures, we are shown a processes for the production of the philosopher's stone in pictorial cryptograms.

Ripley Scroll Hermes with egg shaped vase and 7 stages of Transformation

Figure I: Ripley Scroll (The Yale University version)

Meditating on images, with our knowledge of applied psychology and philosophy, emotionally receiving impressions of the 16th century artists, we hope to comprehend -

An egg shaped vase grey in color, possible of becoming any shape, color or form, full of sperm like tadpole released by a huge green frog presumably in water, as eggs that hatch and through its growth develop limbs and lungs undergoing the most amazing metamorphosis.

Eight of the mandalas, seven depicting alchemical experiments; while the eight is a Biblical scene of Adam and Eve and Tree of Knowledge.

In the center of eight circles are two men, a Pope and a King holding a large black book, most probably a Bible, to which the connecting bands are attached. Surrounded by a mandala repeating words "Soul" "Spirit" "Body". Forming an inner and an outer circle. The line around the outer circle talks about "The Black Sea. The Black Luna. The Black Sol."

Ripley Scroll 2 Adam and Eve and Tree of Life with Serpent Kundalini

Esoteric Teachings of Adam and Eve

The scroll continues exploring the story of Adam and Eve, they stand in water surrounded by 7 alchemists with their transformational processes.

At the top of the tree of knowledge is a naked dragon tailed woman with "Speritu" encrypted on her, holding a child with "Anima" hanging from the branches caressing the naked boy; followed by Adam with a sign of Sun and Eve who worships Moon, standing beside the Tree of Knowledge, observed by the serpent and alchemists.

This scene is in the center of Sun and Moon, facing each other, each with feathers.

Tree of Life and Four (4) Elements

The Tree is held by a strong Man with "Corpus" scripted who stands in the middle surrounded with an angel that is "Spiritus" and an enchained "Anima" (Soul). The man is in a fort with four corner stones: depicting 4 elements: Earth, Air, Fire and Water.

At the very foundation of the image is a dragon eating the frog.

Ripley's words are "The Red Lune. The Spirit of Water. Red Sol. The Red Sea."

Note the eagle has a man's head, and is crowned as a King. Above the eagle is a sun image. Between them drops of water.

Ripley's poetry tells us of:

"The Red Lion. The Green Lion. The bird of Hermes."

"The Red Sea. The Red Sol. The Red Elixir Vitae."

"Red Stone. White Stone. Elixir Vitae. Luna in Crescent…"

"You must make Water of the Earth, and Earth of the Air, and Air of the

Fire, and Fire of the Earth..."

Placing Ripley in time and space of the 15th century you will forgive him for the obscurity of his poetry, since he tried to depict the mystery of an alchemy process of transforming Metals to Gold, at the time when Alchemists were totally impressed by evolving chemistry, observing reactions of various elements to each other.

The most amazing science of chemistry evolved while these researchers were in the midst of their various alchemical experiments.

Ascending the Spiral of Consciousness we realize how we relate to each other in our drive for Goodness.

The Universe's Micro and Macro Cosmos is at our feet searching to manifest as deeper knowledge and understanding of our little Self within Conscious Living with all the sentient beings on our little planet Earth.

Whether you are an atheist, Muslim, Christian or a Hindu in your search for God / Goodness you will know this to be true, there was never a special race of Humans who embodied all the virtues of this world. No matter how sincerely the Kings of our past insisted on inherited DNA hierarchies dividing human race into groups or Castas with the most unfortunate Karmic unwritten laws in India, the Lady Science still hasn't discovered a gene of leadership that could create a capable Ruler.

It is the family, society and friends that guide our children's goodness towards the self-confident and inspiring youth.

4 elements and Rituals from Around the World

It has all started and in its puzzling complexity ends with the worship of God (in Arabic the name for God is AlaH) or divine, with its omnipresent Cosmic entity, in Taoism known as Tao, materialised through trinity of forces (in Hindhuism known as rajas, satwas and tamas) within four elements of Gaia: earth, water, sun, and air.

In their wisdom Chinese philosophers and ancient sages, even managed to further refine them deviding the manifestations of earth into wood and metal, exploring the dance of five instead of four elements. Within the western worlds, inside the works of greatest philosophers, mystics and artists we find this wisdom sparkled knowledge.

Role Models and Mysticism within Art Leonardo da Vinci

Following our drive for goodness and consciousness manifestations, we are 100% sure that if we follow the Role Models our lives will flourish.

Humanity has developed a strong forceful urge to follow the best in the class: the best of scientists, the best of educators, the best of ancestors, the best of the religious followers, Gurus – an Indian man would tell you.

Abusing this noble urge many Kings, read: Churches have offered us (Humanity) a number of lunatics to follow confusing them with "Saints", so our kids will go into wars while they were able to use "killing" as a hypnosis tool with the best of our youths.

Acting as behavioral models, the role models do influence our goal setting and represent the highest potent possibility within our lives. Within our minds they create an inspirational force that influences us throughout our journey, increasing our motivational drive.

Manipulating our drive towards goodness, towards the Role Models, now we have our children following Pop Stars, Actors and TV personalities, whose job is presenting oneself in the most likeable of ways. If the most likeable way is rebellion, they shall give you rebellion, if the most likeable way is truthfulness they shall give you truthfulness.

If we consciously understand this huge drive to follow Role Models, we will be following the likes of Socrates, Plato, Yogananda, Pythagoras, Rumi, Dante, Giordanno Bruno, Bach, Nikola Tesla, Leonardo da Vinci, Patanjali, Leo Tolstoy, Jung, Sri Aurobindo Lao Tzu and St Teresa but following their lives was at times hugely difficult

Spiritual Role Models and Leonardo da Vinci

"During the time of Leonardo... we officially as lunatics marched into the Age of Reason. Our Universities flourished, manuscripts that were for centuries exclusively passed from one monk to the other, were finally discovered, and freely or in secret passed amongst the geeks thirsty of knowledge. In Leonardo. we meet an ideal 'Renaissance man', an all-round genius, a painter, a sculptor, a scientist, an architect, a philosopher and a spiritual teacher with ideas that are far ahead of his time. Leonardo is an inventor with the mind set deep in the future..."

A-Ma Alchemy of Love, 17th century China by Nataša Pantović

Leonardo was the illegitimate son of a respected lawyer, Messer Piero Frosino di Antonio da Vinci, and he was raised within his household since he was five years old.

At the time of virtually no Universities, his father's home schooling gave him an amazing training in music, art, biology, Latin and mathematics, and when he was 14 he became an apprentice in the studio of the prominent Florence artist Verrocchio, a dream training opportunity of all the artists of his time.

His studies with the best in the Europe's center of art Florence, lasted seven years giving him a full exposure to drawing, painting and sculpting. Apart from being a scientist, a researcher, Leonardo was also an accomplished musician playing the lyre and the flute.

Leonardo da Vinci, the Portrait of a Man in Red Chalk, painted in 1512, when Leonardo da Vinci was 60+ and living in France, in Biblioteca Reale, Turin

If you know anything about true art or mysticism, you will know that both are synonyms for a life-long research and devotion to beauty.

It is our Kings, Governments and Churches that have in the past sponsored true art praying their fame will stay with us for eternity.

Leonardo was famous for drawing forward and backward with opposing hands simultaneously, he left many backwards written texts notebooks that could be read only with a mirror. Bill Gates owns the only copy of da Vinci's 72 page manuscript known as the Codex Hammer. The notebook was sold in the mid-1990s for nearly $40 million. The topics within the hand-written manuscript include - the diffusion of light, a study of hydrodynamics, etc.

In art, exploring the portraits of various geniuses whose consciousness manifestations are divine, it is the soul's contact we seek when we look into the eyes of a portrait.

Mystical Art of Leonardo's Monna Lisa

Leonardo was commissioned to do this work in 1503.

A contemporary researcher has discovered a note in a 1477 printing of the ancient Roman philosopher Cicero, a note written by Leonardo's contemporary Agostino Vespucci, saying that Leonardo was at that time working on a portrait of Lisa del Giocondo. The Italian name for the painting, was La Gioconda, meaning "the joyful lady".

Although da Vinci began the work on this masterpiece while living in Italy, he did not finish it until he moved to France in 1517 at King Francois I's request. The French king acquired the portrait and displayed the painting in his Fontainebleau palace. The painting is now on the permanent display at the Louvre Museum in Paris since 1797.

Mona Lisa by Leonardo da Vinci 1517 Louvre Museum Paris

If your soul has a deep passion, you will know this statement to be Truth you will be very sensitive about your devotion, as an artist you will never release a painting, as a writer you will forever write your book, as a musician you will never compose believing your skill is not yet perfect.

If your finances (read state support or family wealth) have allowed you to make a research your life-long focus you will be obsessed with beauty, life and Universe, you will observe stars, people, micro and macro Cosmic manifestations, and you will not be infatuated by own-self but find others hugely interesting.

Not gossiping but admiration will be the energy that flows through your vanes.

Combining this with improving your skills, we now have more than 30 years of life-span (that was the norm in our past) you will joyfully embrace the research in any discipline. So, when the life-forces are against you and you feel physically, mentally or emotionally sick you will use this as a further opportunity to research your body, brain or emotions.

"Art is never finished, only abandoned" Leonardo da Vinci

Mona Lisa was stolen in 1911 with French newspapers reporting the story worldwide. It was returned to the Louvre two years later, with the whole world cheering.

Picasso was under suspicion for the theft.

Also the officials briefly arrested poet Guillaume Apollinaire, who said that the painting should be burned. In 1956 in two separate attacks, one person threw acid at the painting, and another attacked it with a rock...

Having experienced the mystical knowledge within the works of Leonardo, we are left with an impression that there is nothing else to be done or said for eternity. However we face a challenge to explore and re-invent art beyond Leonardo or within the literacy world to write after the likes of Tolstoy or to explore consciousness beyond the works of Jung.

Superstition

There is no deeper enemy to any scientific or creative thinking to the Superstition, so the protection of our Temples became our major hustle all throughout our history.

Protecting a Temple from the destruction, no matter what religion it belongs to, has not yet become our mind-set.

Black-mailing other religious groups with the destruction of their Temples is still a major war strategy. Do you ever wonder why?

The Greek Parthenon is an ancient temple on the Athenian Acropolis, in Greece, dedicated to the goddess Athena, built in 450 BC, when the Athenian Empire was at its peak.

During early 180s Lord Elgin, the British ambassador to the Ottoman Empire, that was occupying the Christian Greece at the time, removed about half of the Temple and transported it to Britain. The oldest ancient Greek temple is now on display in the British Museum in London, together with the full set of Egyptian mummy's graves taken from Egypt.

The political ambiance and religious systems of the time let them change hands with no major upheaval or revolution, at the time there were too few scientists or conscious good men fighting for these sacred items to remain in Greece or Egypt. Since the early 1980s, Greek governments have disputed the British Museum legal title to these most precious antique sculptures...

Now what you probably don't know is that the great limestone rock with the Neolithic remains were discovered on the slopes of the Acropolis Greece, indicating a Temple on the hill from at least 2,800 BC.

The earliest known Hellenistic structures, the one dedicated to Athena dates back to the 600 BC, replacing the previous Megalithic Temple Structure, followed by a Christian Church and a Mosque built on the very exact same sacred spot...

Learning from different Spiritual Traditions

Spiritual Christian, Muslim and Jewish Centre Jerusalem is a city in the Middle East, located between the Mediterranean and the Dead Sea.

It is considered holy to the three major monotheist religions: Judaism, Christianity, and Islam. Both Israel and the Palestinian Authority claim Jerusalem as their capital. During its history, Jerusalem has been destroyed a number of times, and captured and recaptured 44 times.

King Solomon, commissioned the building of the First Temple, 1st millennium BC, making it of central importance for the Jewish people. Christians within the New Testament talk about Jesus's crucifixion there.

In Islam, Jerusalem is the third holiest city, after Mecca and Medina and Muhammad made his Night Journey there, ascending to heaven where he speaks to God, according to the Quran.

Having an area of only 1 square kilometers the Old City is home to the Temple Mount, Dome of the Rock and al-Aqsa Mosque, and the Church of the Holy Sepulchre

.

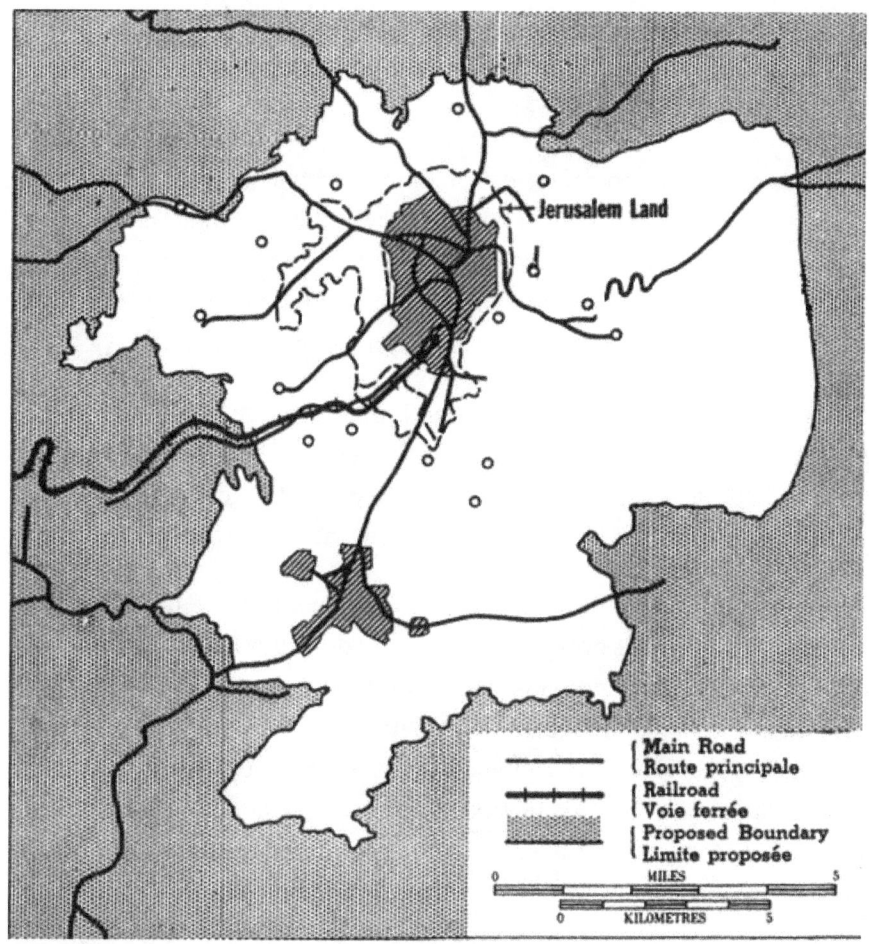

Bethlehem as the ancient center of Christianity was re-built by Empress Helena, in 328 AC, the first of seven wives of the Roman Caesar Constantius, mother of Constantine the Great (who was born in Niš, today's Serbia) historically referred to as the "First Christian Emperor".

Saint Helena was born "the lowest of commoners", most likely a Gypsi, that had no formal education. Already old, she was so impressed by the story of Jesus that in 326 AC, she undertook a trip to the holy places in Jerusalem commissioning the building of two churches, the Church of the Nativity at the site of Christ's birth, and the Church of Eleona, where Jesus' tomb in Jerusalem was. These two places became the holiest places in Christian worship. The exact sites were confirmed by "visions".

Constantine the Great's capital of the Western Roman Empire (West of Rome) was Constantinople (now Istanbul) for more than a thousand years. This Kingdom is now referred to as the Byzantine Empire.

This was such an important area for all the spiritual pilgrims that around the 800 AC, a forged Roman imperial decree (the document called: The Donation of Constantine) by which he is transferring the authority over the "Western Roman Empire" - read Byzantine Empire, to the Pope. This was before the divide in to Catholic and Orthodox Christianity.

Life flourishes with the sun and water. If our homes face "South" eternal sunshine comes to our doors. Yet polarizing our little Planet Earth, we now unfortunately have South that is very poor and North that lives in luxury (the countries that are an exception just prove this rule).

If you live within Gaia's north you have implemented free health and education for all. This brings us to the statistic of 50% of people over 25 with the University degree in Russia that had a huge Government investment in human resources that is now paying off, or in Korea, in Switzerland, Germany or Scandinavia, the richest countries in Europe, around 50% of the University graduates in the US, and 35% in the UK that still protects the combination of Public and Private model of education.

If you are born anywhere in the poor South, and you are reading this, you most probably come from a rich family, like the Buddha who was a son of the King, who shared his wisdom enlightening minds of Gaia 2,000 years ago, or you truly believe in research, beauty and creative thought so you as Leonardo da Vinci has done, made them a center of your life-long research.

If you are in the Vatican State, you will know that just the Sistine Chapel in Rome is visited yearly by 6 million visitors, the museum generates around $87 million from ticket revenue and another $30m from merchandising.

Spiritual Paths

We in the Mediterranean countries see Northerners as more of Yang, or individualistic characters, while in the country like the UK and Scandinavia, North is reserved for the warmer, Yin type of personality, Scottish, while the South is where Englishmen live. When applied, in the European far North, the „north" and „south" as mystical experiences of the ancient Taoist Chinese spiritual system of knowledge are reversed. The medieval English alchemists, Masons, Rosicrucian, mystical Christian practitioners will tell you all about this reversals that confused many during the mid-ages.

In sociology, we acknowledge the difference between the Eastern and Western worlds. Cultural rather than geographical divide, we mentally associate Asia with the East, and Australia, Europe, and America with the West. Some scholars would define Russia as East, and Islamic nations regard predominantly Christian nations as the West. Hinduism, Buddhism, Taoism, and Islam are some common religions of the Eastern worlds. Today our scientists, philosophers, mystics and artists learn from each other, applying science to comprehend the ancient wisdom, Micro and Macro manifestations.

"The same stream of life that runs through my veins night and day runs through the world and dances in rhythmic measures. It is the same life that shoots in joy through the dust of the earth in numberless blades of grass and breaks into tumultuous waves of leaves and flowers. It is the same life that is rocked in the ocean-cradle of birth and of death, in ebb and in flow..."

> Stream of Life, a Bengali poem by Rabindranath Tagore

Albert Einstein says

"I cannot prove scientifically that Truth must be conceived as a Truth that is valid independent of humanity; but I believe it firmly. I believe, for instance, that the Pythagorean theorem in geometry states something that is approximately true, independent of the existence of man."

If you are a woman sincerely practicing any spiritual system of knowledge, do understand with your inner most being that the systems were designed for men, so asserting claims or drawing conclusions is almost impossible!

In Asia, for various reasons, the physical, mental and emotional seclusion was necessary for one to become a Guru.

The main religious scripts of 2,000 years ago up to the 20th century spoke only to the men.

As parents we know of many troubles with the unconscious molded ameba of humanity's struggle, the thought patterns and experiences, that bounce back a decade later, within our kids subconscious behavior patters, are the every day's struggle of each one of us. The bliss of understanding of what angels do, not only surrounded by candle light, but in the midst of a construction site, to protect the purity of the newly born soul, or the bliss of breast-feeding, or higher states of consciousness one can enter putting a child to sleep...

There are many different spiritual paths that we can take: Yoga, Taoism, Christianity, Sufism, etc.

Walking the spiritual path means finding our own relationship with God, Love or Life.

Spiritual not Religious, "Western Roman Empire"

Until recently various Churches and Religions claimed the exclusive right to Spirituality. Religions vailed in mythology ruled the subconscious sphere of our Minds. With the development of science, myths crumbled and the literal explanation of any Vedic or Biblical text became obsolete. In search of Truth we turned towards conscious understanding of symbols and signs, towards comparative studies of various religions and their roots. We turned towards Spirituality not Religion.

Spirituality turns its head towards its predecessor, towards Alchemy, that attempts to understand chemical reactions or micro-biological components.

At the beginning of last century the Theosophical Society researched the secret spiritual teachings of the East and attempted to create a science that researches God, Spirit and Soul's relationship to the Divine.

Anthroposophy, with its founder, Rudolf Steiner, explored the ways that spirituality could be integrated in education, agriculture, or medicine. The gurus and sages of the East developed yoga, chi-gong, meditation and various Spiritual Exercises defining Spirituality as Science many centuries ago.

Spirituality and Souls Materialized on Earth

A unit consciousness called the Self, Soul or Atman (Hindu) materializes within this frame of existence called Earth to experience Life and Death, to understand the form and master its magic. Ancient Egyptians saw the Soul as a Divine Ray, Jews refer to it as the Vital Principle, Hindus see it as a portion of Anima Mundi, or Collective Consciousness or Cosmic Principal called Brahman wondering within Maya's Images of this world.

Lao Tse talks about the spiritual soul that influences the vital soul that is there to animate the body. Christians believe that Holy Spirit communicates with Souls that are the bridge between Divine and Matter.

They all agree that the purpose of Life is evolution of Consciousness. This evolution as the process of personal transformation is called Spirituality.

How to Be a Divergent Thinker or Divergent Activities

To become a Divergent Thinker, we suggest:

- Learn how to ask questions;

The magic of Who, What, and How is already known to a lot of people, yet because we take many things for granted, we usually forget to ask Why.

The question Why? will take us outside the usual boundaries.

The expectations of our superiors, and the world around, us are often "get it done soon" or "should have been done yesterday," and they eliminate the question why.

The different types of questions will lead to different outcomes and they might lead us to very different directions.

"Can you tell me more?"

"How would these insights apply in Malta?"

"Why did you move into that direction?"

"What are the larger issues?"

Sometimes we get obsessed with "trees" observing every single thorn, yet our strength is in the intentional re-focus onto the "forest". Sometimes our "gut feelings" lead us to the unknown, undiscovered territories, and help us explore what our "brain" did not even comprehend.

Give your-self time to explore the art of questioning.

One of the techniques that stimulates various types of questioning is De-Bono 6 Thinking Hats.

De Bono identifies six distinct Hats / ways the brain can be challenged.

In each of these directions the brain identifies and brings into consciousness different ideas and questions: Gut Instinct feelings when putting on an Emotions Red Hat, Black Pessimistic Judgement within a Black Hat, Yellow Optimistic outlook, Managing Blue, Information White with neutral facts, Creativity Green that is outside the box.

Working with colours, different emotional set-up, encourages participants of the discussion to classify their thoughts bringing more clarity to the thinking process.

• Learn to create time and space for meditation and reflection;

• Create bridges to abstract concepts using common experiences, experiments and experiential learning. We should not separate learning and creativity from life; find ways to use nature as a learning setting;

• Brainstorming can be used as a tool that generates a series of random associations, stimulating creative processes;

• Work in collaboration with others – at individual levels, competition frequently kills creativity; working in a group stimulates brain activities.

• Life is a stage, so create acting sets that act out crazy dialogues:

- between historical figures that inspire you,

- between your shadow worlds characters or qualities or

- analyse the scene through the eyes of many different spectators;

• Use creative writing – writing anything that comes to mind about the given subject;

• Utilize both music and art: learning acting with its scenography, filming with its editing, and perspective, drawing and painting with mixing colours and mastering the emotions versus shades or shapes, dancing and its choreography, sculpting, photography with its framing and lighting;

• Practice sports working with tactics, movements and techniques, and teamwork;

• Create Zen space that has stimulating nature art-works using materials created by yourself.

How to Improve Creative Thinking Challenging Existing Beliefs

Challenging the beliefs about the world and the machinery that makes it work is an essential step within the creative process. At all the points of origination of a product, solution, or an artwork, we have a choice to reject our invention and go back to the 'norm'. At all points of the process of 'creation' we are challenged by the 'norm' and we can deny our-own mind-set, energy and feelings.

Creativity and Left and Right Brain Development

Our soul whispers to us constantly. When we understand the power of conscious and subconscious mind and the way the soul communicates with us, we can help ourselves enter the creative flow.

Developing both Left and Right Brain could be essential for Creative Thinkers of our Future.

To purify mind we start with the consciousness that the energy follows thoughts. It is important that we free ourselves of negative beliefs and thoughts, stop gossiping, judging or criticizing and that we work on developing the creative force within us.

Alchemy of Soul by Nuit

artof4elements.com

Will and Love Practiced to invoke her **Majesty Kundalini**
In the world where **Adepts** die & bloom as **Lotuses**
The perfection of Union is Silence
The **Desire for Beauty** within a **Dolphin**
that possesses the **Soul**
keeping it under **Abyss**, giving it **Madness of the Pan**
seeking the **totality of** all possible 'do'-s
jumping into the river full of **streams of thoughts**
Until... The steady sound of a flute Stills Its Mind
Freeing it from its Grossness and Violence
destroying the **illusions** of shame and desires,
and loathsome forms of **Ego-structures**
allowing **Faun to appear and Accept Its True Nature**
Aiming at **Perfection** day after day Purging all of 'I's,
Uniting with 'All'
the Will finally becomes the Self
the Faun transforms into the Unicorn
that knows the **Life of Pure Joy**
and have **only thoughts of clarity and splendour**
Worshiping Silence Ecstasy Transcends Expression
The Soul is Freed

Innovation & Creative Process

When we use our imagination to develop a new idea, the idea is inevitably structured in a predictable way, following already existing concepts. Our schools train us to think as convergent thinkers, aiming for a single, correct solution to a problem, whereas creativity demands divergent thinkers who generate multiple answers to a problem because the aim is to mediate inspiration from the unknown, to create something new.

Learning to access the necessary creativity within our Being is an essential ingredient of the creative flow. Incubation may aid creative problem-solving, because it enables 'forgetting' of existing clues. We are constantly bombarded by 'solutions' so creative minds need to stay isolated from the formulas given by society, seeking for the answers in the most unpredictable places.

A mind should not be thought to passively observe the world, but instead constantly test hypotheses to actively manipulate the environment. The expansion of mind happens when we are open to the new possibilities, when we learn how to be inspired by nature and music and by most versatile forms of art.

Mandala Drawing

Mandala as a Holy Circle

Mandala is a circle that represents Wholeness that represents Divine, our relation to the Infinite, the world within our body and mind and the world outside.

The mandala is used in many spiritual traditions all around the world.

Mandala Meaning with Native American Indians

Native American Indians have medicine wheels and sand mandalas.

The Medicine Wheel or the Sacred Hoop, is a Healing Wheel. It can be an artwork or a construction on the land. The Medicine Wheel respects the four directions: East, South, West, and North represented by a colour (black, red, yellow, and white), elements: fire or sun (spiritual), air (mental), water (emotional), and earth (physical); animals: Eagle, Bear, Wolf, Buffalo, and plants: tobacco, sweet grass, sage, cedar. The ritual used within the Native American ceremonies is a dance in a clockwise direction.

Mandala Meaning and Aztecs

Circular Aztec calendar is in a form of a Mandala

The sacred calendar of the Aztecs of Mexico consisted of a 365-day calendar cycle and a 260-day ritual cycle.

The Aztec sacred calendar called 'xiuhpohualli' divides the days and rituals between the Gods.

The Aztec calendar can be imagined as two wheels connected to each other. One wheel has the numbers 'one' to 'thirteen' written on it. The second wheel has twenty symbols on it. In the merging point, the number one combines with the first symbol. When the wheels start moving number two combines with the second symbol. After fourteen days, the wheel with the numbers shows number one again. The other wheel now shows the fourteenth symbol. After 260 days, the two wheels return to their initial position.

Each day-sign respects a God or an Elemental Force, the provider of the Life Energy for that day. This complex Sacred Calendar gives a reading of the significance of each day.

Mandala Meaning in Tibet

In Tibet, mandalas have complex geometrical shapes and are often used for meditation. Mandalas are sometimes made of sand to emphasize the impermanence of life. When finished, the monks destroy the mandala sweeping it into a river, blessing the water. This action also symbolizes the cycle of life.

Mandalas in Tibet, within the tradition of Tantric Buddhism, are sacred geometric figures that represent the Universe. The word 'mandala' comes from a Sanskrit word that means 'circle'

Monks construct a mandala in a ritual while chanting mantras. In Tibetan Buddhism, contemplation and meditation on a sacred image is central to their spiritual practices and rituals, and a mandala is one of the most sacred of all images.

Taoist Yin and Yang as Mandala

In Asia, the Taoist 'yin and yang' symbol is a mandala (circle representing Universe)

The yin and yang symbol consists of a circle divided into two halves - one white and the other black. Within each half is contained a smaller circle of the opposite colour. The symbol represents Tao (Divine, Universe, God) and the primordial female (Yin) and male (Yang) energy that gives birth to all the manifested world. Yin & Yang are co-existing together dancing their Cosmic Dance continuously transforming one into the other. One cannot exist without the other, as night cannot exist without day, and life cannot exist without death, each contains the essence of the other.

Astrology Zodiac Circle as an Example of a Mandala

The astrology zodiac circle is a circle of Life that maps all the Universal energies in their interplay of forces. A horoscope is a map of heavens: Sun, Moon, and the planets are in a dynamic relation to each other at a specific time, viewed from a specific place on Earth. There are 12 astrological signs with their planets and each sign and constellation of planets has its own particular energy pattern that influences people on Earth.

The astrology zodiac circle is an attempt to understand Universal Laws as manifested on Earth, to comprehend God and its manifestation. The astrology zodiac circle shows the Earth at the centre with the planets around it.

Mandala Meaning and Yoga

In the yoga practices mandala is used to support meditation. Different types of mandalas are used to represent and worship different Gods. Mandala usually has an image that inspires the Spiritual Growth and self development. One of the example is: Sri Yantra or Chakra ('holy wheel') that is a drawing of nine interlocked triangles in a circle, radiating out from the central point. It represents the creation of the Universe and the union of Masculine and Feminine Divine.

Jung about Meaning of Mandalas

Jung mandala meaning 'The "squaring of the circle" is one of the many archetypal motifs which form the basic patterns of our dreams and fantasies... Indeed, it could even be called the archetype of wholeness'... The mandala really is: 'Formation, Transformation, Eternal Mind's eternal recreation'.

About Mandalas, from 'Mandalas', C. G. Jung.

'Very ancient magical effects are hidden in this symbol for it derives originally from the 'enclosing circle', the 'charmed circle', the magic of which has been preserved in countless folk customs. The image has the obvious purpose of drawing a sulcus primigenius, a magical furrow around the centre, the templum, or temenos (sacred precinct), of the innermost personality, in order to prevent 'flowing out', or to guard by apotropaeic means against deflections through external influences.

The magical practices are nothing but the projections of psychic events, which are here applied in reverse to the psyche, like a kind of spell on one's own personality. That is to say, by means of these concrete performances, the attention, or better said, the interest, is brought back to an inner, sacred domain, which is the source and goal of the soul and which contains the unity of life and consciousness. The unity once possessed has been lost, and must now be found again.'

Jung Quote about Mandala, Intro to the Secret of the Golden Flower

'If the fantasies are expressed in drawings, symbols appear which are chiefly of the so-called mandala type. 'Mandala' means a circle, more especially a magic circle, and this symbol is not only to be found all through the East but also among us. Mandalas are amply represented in the Middle Ages. The early Middle Ages are especially rich in Christian mandalas, and for the most part show Christ in the centre, with the four evangelists, or their symbols, at the cardinal points. This conception must be a very ancient one, for the Egyptians represented Horus with his four sons in the same way.'

'Later there is to be found an unmistakable and very interesting mandala in Jacob Boehme's book on the soul. This latter mandala, it is clear, deals with a psycho-cosmic system strongly coloured by Christian ideas. Boehme calls it the 'philosophical eye', or the 'mirror of wisdom', which obviously means a summa of secret knowledge.'

Jung about Christian Mandalas, Intro to Secret of the Golden Flower

According to Jung, mandala is a magic circle, the symbol of the Self, formed by archetypal forces of the unconscious that the artist is not aware of during the creation of the work. The symbols and images come from the collective unconscious, these are primordial images, which reside in each one of us.

Mandala and the Flower of Life

A symbolism of Flower of Life has deep spiritual meaning. Its form is a mandala that consists of multiple evenly-spaced, overlapping circles. The Flower of Life pattern is found in ancient spiritual drawings, as the symbol that depicts the evolution of life within the aspects of space and time. Everything has a mathematical pattern. The Flower of Life carries the pattern of the Universal Life Force. The symbol is found carved in stone within the Temple of Osiris at Abydos, Egypt, possibly representing the Eye of Ra, and later in Phoenician, Asian, Middle Eastern, and Christian art.

Today famous are Leonardo da Vinci's mystical and occult drawings of the Flower of Life. Understanding The Flower of Life help us understand how the Universe works. This symbol could be used during meditations, or as a protection symbol and some use it to improve the quality of their drinking water.

Draw Your Mandala

This exercises is designed to help you experience the benefits of this ancient tool: drawing a mandala.

Get an A3 paper.

You can use any type of colours but do prepare or mix a variety of shades.

Draw a proper circle. Start your Mandala with this circle.

Meditate in front of your circle.

Let the shapes and colours come from the depths of your Soul. Do not hurry. Allow the creation to happen.

Express yourself. Play with colours, play with shapes.

Start drawing from the centre. Let the mandala express itself using this inward movement from the centre of the circle towards its outer parts.

Do not limit your imagination. Do not compete. Just draw. This is your circle. This is your mandala. Let it represent you.

Draw the Mandala and Remember to Enjoy the process, Remember to Play, and Love Your Work of Art!

Finish the Mandala when you feel ready. Allow some time for the drawing to happen. Stay in front of it meditating. Take the proper impression of your new creation.

What does it say? What does it represent? What is the interplay of colours telling you? Is the grey you used very dark? Is there any red within your painting? How about the blue? Write down the thoughts that come to you. Allow the mandala to speak to you about your life.

Share this process with your friends, share your thoughts and feelings.

SPIRITUAL WORK, MEDITATING AND MEDITATION PRACTICE
EXPERIENCING SILENCE

Eternal, flowing, all-encompassing, fully awake, fully aware, entering the Door of No-Time touching the centre of its fullness, feeling the core of its being, floating without a movement, rooted within Non-existence, existing within the breath, spreading piercing Light from every pore, experiencing Her, experiencing Self, experiencing IT, the endless One.

Meditation enters on tip-toes into one's life working through Eternity to reach the mind that is hidden behind a veil of images. Silence starts forming like clouds around arms, chest and throat gathered with spoons of hopes that it will last for-ever. Her voice lingers within the heart, her touch enters with every wind's breeze, her tenderness captures the thoughts' streams, she becomes the first and final embrace, the first and final discovery and the first and final Love.

After you taste her lips, there is nothing else you could long for, after you embraced her, there is nothing else that could warm you, after you desired her there is nothing else you could ask for. You will become her flame, her dust, her wave.

Yoga and Mindfulness

Ever since I fell in love with yoga, 25 years ago, my fascination is fuelled by this amazing Body of Knowledge that flourishes under the umbrella of this Ancient Spiritual Science. 1,000s of years various Yogis devoted their life-times to study the human being, the way we act, behave, or the way our past and present interact within a matrix called our Life and influence our body, mind, and soul.

The experimental and experiential science of Yoga is full of methods and tools that offer to strengthen the willpower, control the mind, work with the emotions and ultimately open the path to enlightenment, giving one as a unit consciousness, a soul, an Atman, an option to merge with Divine Mind, with Cosmic Consciousness, with Brahman, with God.

Covering the wide spectrum of goals, from personal health, through to the improvement of relationships, to the inner peace and happiness, Yoga focusses on all the aspects of this amazing human existence. Materialising as a multi-dimensional art in all the spheres of life, it opens its investigative eye examining:

- symbols and their life within our sub-consciousness (symbolism of chakras),

- sounds and the way our mind relates to the sound vibrations of the Universe

- form (yantras and mandalas) and its mathematical relationship with our Souls and the Universe.

Exploring and experimenting with minute: the control of breath, the play with imagination, work with digestion, fasting, showering, Yoga gives every-single-day's exercises, spiritual tools and suggestions to help us grow into better and more inspiring people.

Yoga and Kundalini

Yogis tremendously respect the Life Force that is within us. Calling it Kundalini, a Yogi, as an experienced doctor or a magician, follows its flow through the Chakras, analysing the qualities and the expression of this Life Force. An anger, for example is a life force directed wrongly through our stomach chakra called Manipura that is coloured red and symbolically represented as a triangle. What a beautiful play of symbolism, knowledge of human nature and imagination! Mistreating the life-force within us with Mal Nutrition or wrong thoughts or emotions may lead to a dis-ease. The disease in turn can be treated by the change of Life Force manifestation.

According to Yogis the happiness can be achieved if the Life Force / Kundalini flows through the Sushuma, the middle channel within our spine, if we balance the wisdom of female intuition with the strength of male action. The major spiritual tool and method to achieve Inner Peace and ultimately Enlightenment is Meditation. Yoga postures (Asanas), breathing (pranayama), vegetarian diet, fasting, nurturing creative thinking, practicing love, compassion, are all there to prepare the body and mind for the magic of the Alchemy of the Soul. Understanding our body and mind: thoughts and emotions, we allow meditation to happen within our Souls and this experience may teach us how to listen to our Soul.

Spiritual Journey Learn to Listen to Your Soul

Body Mind Soul
Train Love   Train Willpower
Respect Gaia   Respect Life
Respect Silence
Conscious Living
Mindful Eating   Mindful Being
Conscious Relationships

Alchemy of Love
Mindfulness Training

OUR MIND

Our mind is constantly busy with thoughts and feelings about our past, present or future. To stop it from useless constant chat, we must learn how to hear this noise, how to become aware of it, and to transform it through concentration into mindfulness.

Taoists with their concept of Yin (unconscious) and Yang (conscious force), Yogis with Ida and Pingala, that are two opposite energy forces that flow through our body, Cabbalists with the female and male side of the Tree of Life, all guide us towards the examination of both: our conscious mind and our or collective unconscious mind.

Researchers say that conscious mind controls our brain only 5% of the day, whereas the subconscious mind has control of our thoughts 95% of the time. A human being has 70,000 thoughts per day.

CONCENTRATION:

With 70,000 thoughts a day and 95% of our activity controlled by the subconscious mind, no wonder that it feels as though we are asleep most of the time. To awake, we need to train self-remembering and mindfulness. Since, mind is in a constant movement, since thoughts attack us from everywhere, to quiet it we need to use its movement, to stop the flow of thoughts, we need to find an object of concentration and focus on it with all our might.

Unconscious or subconscious is vast like an ocean, and the awareness and wakefulness need to be trained for a long time. For a successful training one needs to have a strong Will Power.

It is not natural to wake up at the break of dawn to meditate, and yet it is the most beautiful experience one could have. It is not natural to challenge the existing beliefs, and break the existing patterns, and yet once you manage to do it, you create space for the new patterns to form, the ones that are filled with love, acceptance, knowledge, and you give yourself a chance to spiritually grow.

START WITH SMALL STEPS: REDUCE THE 'MENTAL NOISE' AROUND YOU (SWITCH OFF TV AT BREAKFAST), IMPROVE YOUR SLEEP, WALK TO THE GROSSER, MEDITATE WHEN PUTTING YOUR BABY TO SLEEP...

Exercise your Willpower

OUR WILL-POWER NEEDS TRAINING

Willpower needs to be trained every single day, so that it could be later used in the process of Spiritual Development.

You train your Willpower or Will Power when you challenge your existing structures, when you go against your instincts, against the hunger, when you go against your sleep, when you challenge your limits whatever they are.

Write your-own list of actions for exercising Will Power during the duration of this Course. These are some of our suggestions:

-   do not eat immediately when you are hungry – wait a couple of minutes, challenging your hunger

-   do not sleep immediately when you are sleepy – wait a couple of minutes, challenging your sleep

-   at the end of your shower, use cold water, challenging your comfort zones

-   swim in cold waters

-   wake up early to walk or jog

-   wake up early to meditate

-   run a marathon

-   climb Mont-Everest

-   fast on water for more than 24 hours

-   do not have an orgasm after 11 minutes of sex with your partner but enter into a magic of making love that might last hours

-   do not get angry, even though circumstances are against you

WILLPOWER IS THE BASIS OF ALL SELF DEVELOPMENT WORK

Train your Willpower

With the strong Willpower you will be able to invite the lady Love into your life and let Her rule from the centre of your Heart.

MINDFULNESS EXERCISES: PRACTICE CONCENTRATION

PRACTICE CONCENTRATION: FOCUS ON A CANDLE LIGHT

Do this exercise in the evening. Sit comfortably and lit a candle just in front of you. Observe the flame without moving.

Fix your gaze on the flame. Do not blink.

Stay observing the candle as long as you can. The flame will keep this effort alive for quite a long time.

When you feel that your eyes are tiered, close them, and see the candle within your third eye.

It will be as alive as the real candle, continue focusing on its flame. Repeat the exercise once or twice. End this concentration exercise in about 10-15minutes.

THIS EXERCISE CAN ALSO BE DONE IN A GROUP. FORM A CIRCLE AND PUT A CANDLE IN THE MIDDLE OF 4-5 PEOPLE. DO NOT MOVE, DO NOT TALK, JUST OBSERVE THE FLAME.

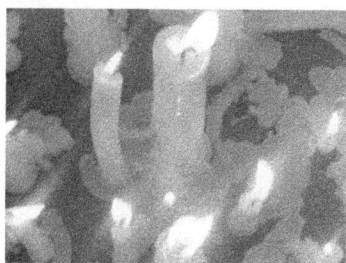

Daily Meditation

Silence is healing. Silence is creative. Silence is necessary. Regular meditation is a way to clear your mind from a clutter of thoughts, a way to train concentration and to focus on specific themes.

CONCENTRATION

Our Mind is constantly active. Seeking stillness within the Mind that is in motion is impossible if you do not use the motion itself. When the surface of a lake is still, we will be able to see, experience, intuitively sense the ocean of our sub-conscious and to tap into the magic of super-conscious. This is impossible when the surface is agitated by waves of our thoughts, emotions, habits, fears.

In order to still our mind we will learn how to understand the body and the influence it has on our mind. The art of meditation is the art of stillness, the art of motion within no-motion, action within no-action, visualization and concentration.

Chose an object of Beauty that inspires you and use it as your object of meditation – a rose, a tree, a crystal, light...

Concentrating our mind on light, love, peace, or pure consciousness, we allow the mind to keep 'busy' while we connect with the source of power, love, peace and knowledge using powerful imagery of positive imagination.

Create your own meditation, and follow it!

Do not Harm

Do not harm yourself or others physically, mentally or emotionally. We hear these simple and powerful words, everywhere. Do not kill. Do not lie. Do not harm other beings on Earth. Stepping into the world of virtues, we come across the magic of the control over thoughts and feelings that are driven by fear, attachment and instincts.

Inspired or Lost within Technology Matrix

We live surrounded by an increasingly complex matrix of impulses allowing strangers of all sorts (TV, media, Internet) interfere in our mental, emotional and spiritual development. Understanding this intricate network and how does the human brain interacts with it is becoming our door to happiness and health.

The self or the personality is a bundle of socially influenced traits that emerges and gets formed gradually. We are shaped by our parents and neighbours, by our religion, the media, by various marketing agendas of major corporations, by our state's politics, by the way we behave or misbehave towards our-own body, our mind, environment, animals and plants, and our planet Earth. So, what would we need to do to understand the importance of a healthy body, to manage our emotions and nurture love for our friends and family, to become aware of how we can make a positive impact on our society or the environment, or discover the purpose of life and ways to be happy?

Negative Effects of Technology on Children

A great deal is known about our behaviour and TV, and our emotions and computer games, because there have been thousands of studies on these subjects. The researchers have all asked the same question: Whether there is a link between exposure to violence (on TV or within a game) and violent behaviour? Most of the studies answered: 'yes – the link is there'. According to the AAP (American Academy of Pediatrics), 'Extensive research evidence indicates that media violence can contribute to aggressive behaviours, desensitization to violence, nightmares, and fear of being harmed.' An average American child will see 200,000 violent acts and 16,000 murders on TV by age 18...

None of us wants to see our children or our loved ones depressed, obese, in front of computers or TV screens at all times, having behavioural problems, being sick, or experiencing attention deficit hyperactivity disorder. However, the rhythm of our lives and our day-today habits might have an adverse effect on our mental health.

Negative Effects of Technology on Society

Human brain does some very sophisticated ordering of its incoming nerve impulses. Any information that we are exposed to becomes knowledge when it is translated and related to the personal experience, to the feelings, or desires. When we look at an image, our perception of an image is coloured by our emotions. There is a reciprocal relationship between the area of the brain responsible for logical thinking and the area that is the seat of our emotion. Within the world of technology, numbers, letters, adverts, 'human brain' has to constantly perform little miracles of de-coding, detachment, de-stress, and de-tox to keep us sane and free of diseases. As we grow older, and stronger in our wish to stay healthy and happy, our need for creativity grows, we constantly luck time to be physically active, to read and reflect, to play, and amongst all, we luck the quality time with our friends and family. The interaction with the NET, with the TV, with the computer has replaced the interaction with nature that in its magic way nurtures our cognitive, emotional, physical and psychological well-being.

Negative Effects of Technology on Communication

A group of friends socializing will have a number of mobiles handy on the table, easily within reach for checking e-mails, showing off photos, or answering a call. This invisible 'best friend' and inseparable 'commodity' could prove to be our 'worst enemy'...

A recent study by Andrew Przybylski and Netta Weinstein of the University of Essex observed couples of strangers discussing a meaningful topic for 10 minutes with or without a cell phone nearby. The pairs who tried to 'connect' in the presence of a cell phone repeatedly reported lower relationship quality and less closeness with the assigned 'chatting' partner. The studies suggest that because of the many 'entertainment' options phones give us they distort our ability to connect with the people right next to us.

"The presence of a mobile phone may orient individuals to thinking of other people and events outside their immediate social context. In doing so, they divert attention away from a presently occurring interpersonal experience to focus on a multitude of other concerns and interests." said the lead researcher Andrew Przybylski.

A study for the Journal of Behavioural Addictions in the US analysed the data from 191 business students from two universities and revealed that students send on average 110 texts a day, or approximately 3,200 messages a month and check their phones 60 times in a typical day. Nomophobia is the term for people who experience anxiety when they have no access to their mobiles.

Negative Effects of Technology on Relationships

An electronic 'connection' interferes with our human relationships. Saying 'I love you' and texting 'I love you' could have completely different connotations based on body language. Discounting the value of nonverbal cues leads to an amazing amount of mis-understandings.

Text messages are used in our romantic and sexual correspondence. A wonderful romantic love letter became obscure. Texting is quick, easy, and convenient and notwithstanding its 160 characters limitation, some people use it to exchange important information with their romantic partner. Messages are often misinterpreted, often edited, forwarded, or written by somebody else. The stress caused by the response expectation is unique for this type of communication. A lack of response to a text message from a potential romantic partner is often deciphered as a form of rejection.

How to Avoid Negative Impact of Technology

So, how to help our minds stay inspired and enthusiastic and our relationships stay healthy?

Limit your time with TV, mobiles and computers;

If you are spending the time with people you really care about, you might want to re-consider the habit of reaching for your phone to reply to a text message or checking your e-mail.

Spend quality time with your loved ones, re-invent your time together: sing, dance, do art together, or explore learning a new language;

Experiment, challenge the existent, and stay curious;

Stay in constant contact with nature.

Main Benefits of Meditation

Why do we meditate?

Through the practice of meditation, we enter a world of soul and spirit, and with patience and training we start yielding results.

Meditation Benefits: Short Term

So, why do we meditate?

Is it for the bliss we feel during an amazing meditation or for the results that we experience after some years of training?

Benefits of Meditation and Thinking Process

Have you noticed that within the thinking process, a thought weaves into another thought, seeking the other. If we listen to our thoughts, and observe the thinking process, we notice that the thought world has its-own inner life. A rose acts upon us when we see its colour, when we smell its fragrance, it influences us through its symbolism, through its beauty, through its existence within our lives, within our art-works, within our gardens for centuries. We tap into the thought form of 'rose adoration'.

It is as though the thoughts are already present when our soul surrenders to their flow and re-create them anew within.

Some thoughts that are inspiring, or moving, act within us like living entities. Meditating upon them, various philosophers and mystics contemplated problems and solutions of the world, universe, and life.

Long Term Benefits of Meditation

Through a proper self-development training of:

- body through nutrition and exercise,
- of mind through meditation, and
- of emotions through exercising virtues

we awake amazing capacities of our Soul and bring into our lives the magic of one-pointed focus in all the areas of life

Benefits of Meditation: Divine Inspiration

We are in a constant search for truth, for beauty, and for wisdom within the creation. Meditating we gain a capability to read and understand synchronicity within one's life.

The next section is spiritual not religious collection of meditations and prayers from around the world that we hope will give you **Divine Inspiration and Creative Divine Impulse.**

9 Most Important Tips to Cultivate Creativity

1. Devote Time to Creativity

Developing the skill of creativity, like with any other skill, needs time. Do devote time to creativity. Honour its flow and its magic. Allow it to become your Life Force. Train Creativity daily.

2. Ask Questions, Stay Curious and Inquisitive, Be Grateful

People who are curious, persistent, who experiment, make mistakes and are willing to take risks have the courage to be creative. The ones who are grateful for what they got know how to appreciate life. Challenge and explore the world around you and always give yourself time and space for reflection. We are constantly bombarded by ready made 'solutions', have courage to be creative.

3. Practice Silence

Creative minds need to stay isolated from the formulas given by society, seeking for the answers in most unpredictable places, within the silence of meditation. The meditation has no thoughts, no feelings, no images. Entering meditation, you enter the pure consciousness.

4. Do not separate learning from Life

Allow Life to be Your Guiding Force into the centre of Creativity. Creativity is a Life Force and a State of Being, if properly respected and trained, it will connect you with the qualities of Love, Inspiration, Beauty.

5. Use the Stream of Consciousness Writing or Write Poetry

Let your soul and intuition express the subtle inner relationships within your life through poetry and stream of consciousness writing. Awake creativity, and imagination through the unobstructed, unstructured early morning writing.

6. Practice Music and Arts

Researches show that artists are more likely to use both hemispheres of their brain. Stay within the Creative Flow. To be creative we choose to be different from everyone else. Learning the skill of creativity is about learning to challenge the existing.

7. Spend Time in Nature

Beauty of any flower pattern connects us with the forever present field of Life Force that has an amazing mathematical intelligence that pulsates through all living beings. Our state of consciousness is very different when we try to cross a crowded street in a metropolis and when we contemplate a shape of a tree in the middle of a mountain path.

8. Challenge Existing Beliefs

Challenge the beliefs about the world and the machinery that makes it work. Ask questions, free your mind and think, research, listen to inspiring people and create your-own opinion.

Challenge existing beliefs, create your-own practice that breaks stereotypes. Walk backwards, become a vegetarian, wear different socks, 'strange' colours, dance in the middle of a street, meditate, say 'hello' to everyone you meet, create your own song, etc.

9. Get Inspired and Share Inspiration within Rich and Stimulating Environments

A mind will expand when we are open to the new possibilities, when we stay full of wonder and when we are inspired by nature, events and people. Share this inspiration further. This is possible if you Live in the Present Moment. Do not separate learning from life; learn constantly, and access the creative flow within you getting inspired from the world around you.

Conscious Creativity Course

Module 1: Inner Child

Objective: To heal and nurture the Inner Child, connecting with past wounds and integrating them into a healthy, balanced adult self.

Week 1: Rediscovering the Inner Child

Exercise 1: Creating a Safe Space for the Inner Child

Goal: Establish a safe mental space where your inner child feels secure and heard.

Instructions:

Imagine a safe, peaceful place where your inner child feels protected. Spend 10–15 minutes in meditation visualizing yourself as a child, asking how they feel and what they need. Write down any insights that arise.

Exercise 2: Dialogue with the Inner Child

Goal: Engage in an inner dialogue to address and heal childhood wounds.

Instructions:

Write a letter from your inner child to your adult self, then reply with compassion from your adult self. Repeat this process over several days to explore deeper healing.

Week 2: Nurturing the Inner Child

Exercise 3: Gestalt Empty Chair Technique

Goal: Revisit emotional experiences and integrate feelings from your inner child. Instructions:

Sit in front of two chairs — one for yourself and one for your inner child. Alternate between both chairs, exploring the emotional needs and perspectives of both the child and adult. Reflect on the insights gained.

Exercise 4: Inner Child Affirmations

Goal: Reaffirm your worth from the perspective of your inner child.

Instructions:

Write positive affirmations from your inner child's perspective (e.g., "I am worthy of love," "I am enough"). Say them aloud each day, visualizing your adult self-offering love to your inner child.

Module 2: Family Relationships

Objective: To improve family dynamics and foster healthier, more conscious relationships within the family unit.

Week 1: Understanding Family Dynamics

Exercise 1: Family Tree Mapping

Goal: Explore and understand the patterns and dynamics in your family lineage.

Instructions:

Draw a family tree, identifying key family members and emotional patterns (love, conflict, communication). Reflect on how these patterns influence your relationships today.

Exercise 2: Gestalt Family Dynamics Exploration

Goal: Explore unconscious dynamics that influence family relationships.

Instructions:

Using the empty chair technique, role-play conversations or conflicts with family members. Alternate between chairs to understand different perspectives and reflect on how this can improve family communication.

Week 2: Strengthening Family Connections

Exercise 3: Steiner's Rituals of Togetherness

Goal: Introduce family rituals that enhance connection and strengthen emotional bonds.

Instructions:

Develop a family ritual (e.g., shared meal, weekly walk) that promotes unity and harmony. Encourage active participation from all members and reflect on how it improves relationships.

Exercise 4: The Six Thinking Hats for Family Problem Solving

Goal: Apply de Bono's Six Thinking Hats to resolve family issues more collaboratively.

Instructions:

Identify a family issue and apply each of the six thinking hats (White, Red, Black, Yellow, Green, Blue) to explore different perspectives. Work as a family to generate solutions.

Module 3: Getting Rich – Business Focus & Success

Objective: Focus on building a successful, mindful, and purpose-driven art business using tools for creative thinking, and strategic planning.

Week 1: Building a Vision for Your Business

Exercise 1: Business Mind Mapping

Goal: Use Divergent Thinking to explore all possibilities for your business.

Instructions:

Create a mind map with your business idea at the center. Branch out to areas like products, target market, financial goals, and personal values.

Identify the most promising ideas and explore them further.

Exercise 2: The Provocation Technique for Business Innovation

Goal: Challenge assumptions and explore new, unconventional business ideas.

Instructions:

Address a current business challenge (e.g., marketing, sales). Use provocative questions (e.g., "What if I gave my product away for free?") to spark new ideas.

Week 2: Strategic Planning for Success

Exercise 3: Setting SMART Goals for Business Success

Goal: Establish clear, actionable goals for your business.

Instructions:

Set 3–5 SMART (Specific, Measurable, Attainable, Relevant, Time-bound) goals. Break each down into smaller tasks, setting deadlines and reviewing progress.

Exercise 4: De Bono's Six Thinking Hats for Business Strategy

Goal: Use the Six Thinking Hats to make informed, balanced business decisions.

Instructions:

Apply the Six Thinking Hats technique to a key business decision (e.g., launching a new product). Reflect on insights gained and implement solutions.

Week 3: Manifesting Abundance

Exercise 5: Visualization for Success

Goal: Use visualization to manifest your business goals.

Instructions:

Visualize your business thriving, clients being happy, and experiencing financial abundance. Make this visualization a daily practice to stay motivated.

Exercise 6: Gratitude Practice for Business Growth

Goal: Foster an abundance mind-set by practicing gratitude.

Instructions:

Keep a gratitude journal, writing down three things you're grateful for each day in relation to your business. Reflect weekly on how this affects your mind-set and business decisions.

Module 4: Art Therapy for Personal Transformation and Creativity

Objective: Use art as a therapeutic tool for self-exploration, emotional expression, and creativity enhancement.

Week 1: Expressing Emotions through Art

Exercise 1: The "Here and Now" Artwork

Goal: Use art to express emotions without judgment.

Instructions:

Without any intention to "make art," allow yourself to express your current emotions through colour, shape, or form. Reflect on what emotions surfaced and any recurring patterns in your artwork.

Exercise 2: Art as a Mirror of the Inner World (Gestalt Approach)

Goal: Use art to explore unconscious feelings and experiences.

Instructions:

Create an art piece representing a symbol that resonates with you (e.g., tree, animal). Engage in a Gestalt dialogue with the symbol, reflecting on the insights it provides.

Week 2: Exploring Archetypes and Symbols through Art

Exercise 3: The Shadow in Art (Jungian Approach)

Goal: Explore and integrate your Shadow aspects through creative expression.

Instructions:

Represent a shadow trait (e.g., anger, insecurity) through art. Reflect on the insights gained from embracing this hidden part of yourself.

Exercise 4: Archetypal Figures in Your Art (Jungian)

Goal: Explore key Jungian archetypes shaping your life and creativity.

Instructions:

Create an artwork representing an archetype (e.g., The Hero, The Wise Old Man). Reflect on its role in your life and creativity, and how you can embody or learn from it.

Week 3: Creative Blocks and Healing

Exercise 5: Visualizing Blockages and Releasing through Art

Goal: Uncover and dissolve creative blocks using art.

Instructions:

Visualize your creative block as an object, then create an artwork representing the blockage. Shift focus to how you can transform it into something positive, and reflect on the release process.

Exercise 6: Inner Child Art Therapy (Gestalt and Jungian Approach)

Goal: Connect with your inner child through creative expression and healing.

Instructions:

Create art representing your inner child, and engage in a dialogue with this part of yourself to identify what it needs. Reflect on how to nurture and care for your inner child.

Module 5: Dream Analysis for Creativity

Objective: Unlock creativity and self-awareness by exploring dreams and unconscious material using Gestalt and Jungian methods.

Week 1: Dream Journaling and Symbolism

Exercise 1: Keeping a Dream Journal

Goal: Begin analysing your dreams to uncover patterns and symbols.

Instructions:

Record your dreams each morning. Look for recurring themes, symbols, or figures. Reflect on their possible connections to your waking life.

Week 2: Active Imagination (Jungian Technique)

Exercise 2: Dialogue with Dream Figures

Goal: Engage with the unconscious through active imagination.

Instructions:

Choose a significant figure from your dreams and visualize them. Engage in conversation, asking them for insights. Record the dialogue for deeper understanding.

Week 3: Dream Incubation for Creative Insights

Exercise 3: Dream Incubation (Jungian and Gestalt Approach)

Goal: Use dreams to solve creative challenges.

Instructions:

Focus on a creative problem before sleeping. Write down an intention or question, and reflect on any dream insights upon waking.

Week 4: Integrating Dream Insights into Daily Life

Exercise 4: Dream Symbol Collage (Gestalt Technique)

Goal: Integrate dream insights through a visual representation.

Instructions:

Create a collage of symbols from your dreams and place it somewhere visible to remind yourself of their meaning. Reflect on how these insights influence your life and creativity.

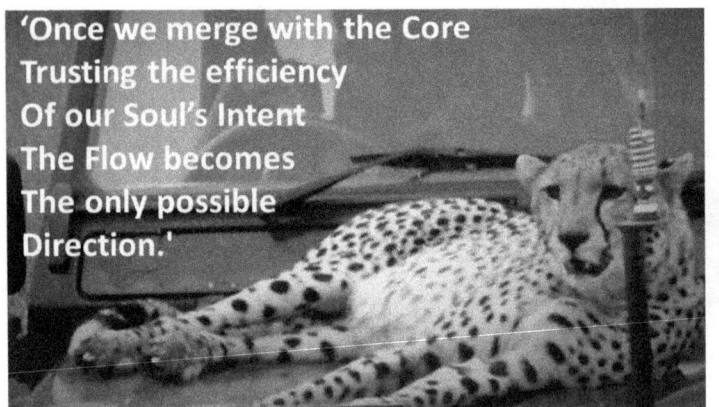

Art of 4 Elements by Nuit   www.artof4elements.com

ABOUT THE AUTHOR

Nataša Pantović MSc Economics
Maltese-Serbian Novelist, Adoptive Parent, and Ancient Worlds' Consciousness Researcher

Nataša Pantović is a renowned author, educator, and researcher with a deep passion for exploring ancient philosophies and consciousness. Born in 1968 in Belgrade, Serbia, she has built a diverse career, transitioning from a successful business development executive to a published author and consciousness researcher. With a background in Economics and over 25 years of experience in management consulting and executive training, Nataša has worked with leading organizations like KPMG, Deloitte, Reeds, and the Government of Malta.

Her career journey has taken her across the UK, Holland, and Malta, where she inspired countless professionals and leaders to reach beyond their self-imposed boundaries. Nataša has organized six large Body, Mind, and Spirit Festivals and participated in panels at international conferences, including the International Vegetarian Festival and a 10-day event about Neolithic Temples. Her passion for empowering others is evident in her volunteer work, which includes building a school in a remote Ethiopian village.

As an adoptive mother, Nataša has shared her powerful and unusual journey of motherhood as a single parent, raising two children while continuing to pursue her writing and research. Since founding Artof4Elements five years ago, she has published two historical fiction novels and seven non-fiction works, blending ancient wisdom with modern mindfulness techniques.

Her research interests focus on the consciousness of Ancient Europe and the intersection of applied psychology and philosophy, from Taoism to Jungian theory. Nataša's unique approach to mindfulness is deeply influenced by her exploration of Western ancient Greek philosophers, and she often blends these influences with Eastern concepts of self-awareness.

An advocate for living a life of purpose and potential, Nataša has appeared in the Sunday Times, where she discussed her unusual treatment of "Mindfulness," explaining that it's not about quick fixes, but about aligning with one's soul to reach the highest potential.

Nataša is fluent in English, Serbian, all Balkan Slavic languages, Maltese, and Italian. She is dedicated to fostering a more conscious world, where individuals can think creatively, appreciate art, and thrive without harming others or the planet. Books published:

* "Co-operative Laws Contracts" in Serbian (1991)
* "A-Ma Alchemy of Love | or Playing the Glass Bead Game with Pythagoras" (2018)
* "Art of 4 Elements | Discover Alchemy through Poetry" with Christine Cutajar, Jason V. Lu and Jeny Caruana (2015)
* "Mindful Being Course| towards Mindful Living' (2016)
* "Conscious Parenting | Mindful Living Course for Parents ' (2017) with Ivana Milosavljević
* "Tree of Life | a Journey into the Field of Dreams" (2018)
* "Conscious Creativity | Ancient Europe's Mindfulness Meditations" (2019)
* "Spiritual Symbols | with Their Meanings" (2019)
* Metaphysics of Sound | In Search of the Name of God" (2021)
* 999: Playing the Glass Bead Game with Pythagoras" (2022)

www.ingramcontent.com/pod-product-compliance
Lightning Source LLC
Chambersburg PA
CBHW020004050426
42450CB00005B/309